The Vurger Co.
at home

The Vurger Co.
at home

80 SOUL-SATISFYING,
INDULGENT & DELICIOUS
RECIPES

Harper
Collins

Contents

Our Story

NEIL AT OUR FIRST
EVER MARKET STALL

That mission began with Neil and me selling burgers at market stalls, events, festivals and parties up and down the country to build The Vurger Co. name. At the time, we both had to support the growth of the brand, which took a lot of time, effort and money. In those early years we both worked full time Monday to Friday in our day jobs to support the market stalls, then we would prep on the Saturday and sell in the market on the Sunday.

We introduced items onto our menu that were not readily available across London in their vegan form: mac 'n' cheese, shakes, multiple burger options and lots of sides.

Pretty soon, people were travelling across the city to get their Vurger fix!

**THE FIRST
VURGERS MADE**

We are so proud to be able to introduce *The Vurger Co. At Home* recipe book, enabling everyone worldwide to make fun and delicious plant-based recipes at home.

The Vurger Co. began in 2016 with a clear mission from the beginning: to revolutionise fast food through the power of plants.

When we started out it was rare to be able to access any type of quick service food outlet that was completely dedicated to plant-based ingredients. We wanted to change the perception that people had at the time and become the new wave of casual dining; making it seriously delicious and, of course, available to everyone, without judgement.

We then teamed up with the incredibly talented chef, Gaz Oakley.

After meeting at one of our early pop-up events in 2016, and, of course, all being Welsh, Neil and I immediately knew this was going to be a partnership for life. Gaz creates the most incredible recipes, that just so happen to be totally plant-based and seriously delicious. We teamed up for several collaborations over the years, eventually leading to Gaz becoming our official Executive Chef between 2018 and 2020. Gaz continues to be an incredible part of our team, with ongoing support and input – even contributing unique recipes to this book. We are so grateful for his support and love throughout the years and we couldn't have done it without him!

Our brand has changed a lot since those early days. Back then, we knew we would need a lot of support to make our food the best that it could be and must credit the early pioneers of this space, who really supported and helped us when we were starting out. First and foremost, **Amanda Cohen**, who is the James Beard-nominated chef and owner of Dirt Candy, the award-winning vegetarian restaurant on New York City's Lower East Side. Also, **Andrew Dargue**, chef and owner of Vanilla Black, which was a trailblazing restaurant in London's Holborn that showcased just how amazing vegetables can be. And chef and author, **Chloe Coscarelli**, who became the first vegan participant to win a culinary competition on television (Cupcake Wars) and was named in the 2017 Class of 30 Under 30 by Forbes. Chloe joined us at a Los Angeles festival in May 2018 where we sold our collaboration burger to thousands of attendees. This level of support for what was, at the time, a small brand really showcased Chloe's level of passion for her craft.

At that moment in time the London vegan food scene was just starting to wake up, with more options popping up around the city. We managed to open our first bricks and mortar restaurant in Shoreditch, in March 2018, after a successful crowdfunding campaign. Much love and thanks to Morgan Masters for all her support and hard work in making this happen.

Our second store then opened in Canary Wharf in November of the same year. We traded with two sites fully operational over seven days a week, right up to the start of the global pandemic in 2020. Despite the challenges of the pandemic lockdowns, we opened our Brighton store in July 2020 and went on to open our fourth store in Manchester in April 2022. Opening four stores in as many years with a pandemic going on for two of those years is no mean feat! Our condiments range also launched during the pandemic, in March 2020. It was available directly on our website, via multiple retailers across the UK, as well as internationally in the US and Middle East. As a brand, it was so important to us that our customers could recreate their favourite Vurger specials at home, in spite of the obvious challenges brought about by the pandemic.

Elly Smart, our Head of Development, worked non-stop on developing the best flavours and textures for our mayos, which were unique both in the way they were made, but also in the way they tasted. Mayo had never been so good! We are all so proud of our range of sauces, and incredibly grateful that they are available across several continents.

Elly and her Development Manager, Carolyn Mwarazi, are the masterminds and driving force behind this wonderful book, and all the delicious recipes you will hopefully enjoy creating at home. It has been a complete joy putting all of these creations together in one place and, of course, tasting everything along the way. We couldn't be prouder of these two amazingly talented and creative chefs that we are so lucky to get to work with every day.

We have put a great amount of energy and innovation into making sure we remained unique in our offering, by constantly pushing the boundaries of what we can do with the ingredients we use. We are incredibly proud of this. Our coconut bacon, our caramel, our shake base, our crispy spiced jackfruit pieces, our vegan honey... the list goes on. The best part for us is that these are all recipes originally used in our restaurants.

This book is a treasure trove of top tips from our creators, collaborators and incredible team, including a unique insight into how we come up with new recipes throughout the book.

We want to say a massive thank you to every single person who has supported us throughout our journey. To say we wouldn't be here without you is an understatement. We really hope you love this book, as much as we have all enjoyed making (and taste-testing) it!

Much love,
Rachel and Neil x
Co-founders, The Vurger Co.

PICK UP

ORDER

The
Vurger
Co.

THE VURGER CO. RESTAURANT
IN MANCHESTER

About This Book

The Vurger Co. At Home is absolutely crammed full of easy-to-follow plant-based recipes for everyone. We have been innovating in the plant-based world since 2016 – creating tempting, delicious and accessible food for all through our restaurants across the UK.

We couldn't wait to put together all of the collective hints, tips and tricks that we have learnt over the years and share these with our favourite people – you!

We have a gorgeous Brunch section, packed full of recipes you would be so proud to share with your friends on any lazy weekend. We also have our Lighter Lunches section, which is the perfect solution to creating amazing plant-based lunches at home. Try out our team favourite, the Ultimate Caesar Salad, or quick-and-easy salad toppers, ideal for adding a gorgeous crunch to any recipe.

Our Fakeaway section is truly where we couldn't wait to share some insider secrets and ways to team different dishes to create your favourite takeaway at home. We have recipes to create your ideal 'chicken'-style takeaway, a major focus on potatoes in all their glory, and incredible sub and slider recipes that will blow your friends and family away. Of course, we have shared three absolute staple burger recipes, showcasing some golden oldies and some new ways to work with incredible plant-based ingredients too.

Then enter the Party Bites section, where we have gone all out to make sure you can create the most epic plant-based party right in your own home. Trust us, these are winning recipes for any age, go wild!

We have devoted so much time and attention to our Sweet Treats section. When testing these recipes, so many people could not believe the recipes were vegan at all, they are so seriously delicious. We had people diving in and coming back for more. We'd call that a big win!

Finally, this wouldn't be a Vurger Co. book without a section on sauces. This makes up a huge part of our business so we can't wait for you to give these a go, from our classic Ranch to exclusive recipes like our Bacon Jam, there is something here for everyone.

To make it simple for you to make gluten-free recipes, we've added these two symbols throughout the book:

GF The recipe is gluten-free

GFO The recipe can easily be made gluten-free by following the options given in the recipe list

All in all, we are incredibly proud of each section. We truly hope our hints, tips and tricks along the way, teamed with the unique recipes created by our team, will give everyone the chance to become the most incredible plant-based chef of the future

We're all counting on you!
Thank you so much for your support
and happy cooking.

With much love
The Vurger Co. team

Our Food

Feeding your soul with our 100% plant-based menu since 2016.

Our ethos has always centred around revolutionising fast food through the power of plants – a mission that back in 2016 was much less accepted than now! Over the years we have gone from making all of our burger patties purely from legumes and vegetables, to adding in some meat replacement options to suit every palate. We never sacrifice flavour and therefore aim to source the highest quality ingredients with as few additives as possible, making most items centrally in-house to closely monitor the quality.

As a vegan food brand, we are extra conscious of all ingredients we use and source, ensuring that they in line with our ethos of limiting the harm we do to the environment in the production or procurement of products. We aim to limit the use of products that have a high carbon footprint (such as avocados) and aim to keep our products as locally sourced as possible.

We are also passionate about reducing plastic waste. All of our restaurant food packaging is compostable and we have a dedicated compostable waste management partner to ensure we are not contributing to landfill.

Our development team are constantly working on producing new specials for our restaurants, which are researched and taste-tested (hardest part of the job!) before making their way into our restaurants. We have launched countless new specials since 2016 and take such pride in every new product – a true labour of love from start to finish.

We have really taken the time to ensure the love, care and attention shown in creating every restaurant recipe has translated to every recipe in our book.

HUNNY 'CHICKEN' BURGER

Essential Equipment

We have tried and tested our recipes in many home kitchens and have put together a key equipment list, as well as some additional items that will ensure maximum success with minimal effort.

Kitchen Essentials

Mixing bowls
Frying pan
Saucepans
Balloon whisk
Chopping board
Baking trays
Kitchen knives – sharpened
Potato masher
Muffin tray
20-cm (8-inch) cake pan
Sugar thermometer
Ice cube tray
Heatproof bowls
Zester
Foil and parchment paper
Grater
Airtight storage containers
Sieve

Additional Equipment

Air fryer
High-speed blender
Stick blender
Hand-held electric whisk
Skillet
Pestle and mortar
Microwave
Nut-milk bag
Waffle maker

We really rely on these kitchen staples when making our food at home. We have also become completely addicted to our air fryer! However, please remember that if you don't have an air fryer the items can be just as easily fried in oil in a pan or even popped into the oven. We try to provide alternatives, where possible, throughout the book.

Ingredient Guide

We know some vegan ingredients might seem unfamiliar and a little daunting, but we absolutely love how plant-based food pushes you out of your comfort zone to discover new and exciting flavours. Here is a list of ingredients used in this book that you may or may not have heard of before. We would highly recommend giving them a try!

Dairy alternatives

Non-dairy milk

We are surrounded with vegan milk alternatives now, so for all recipes simply choose your favourite one. We love oat and cashew milks, as they aren't usually sweetened and add great creaminess to dishes.

Non-dairy butter

Again, you will be spoilt for choice when choosing a vegan butter in the supermarkets. We try to find options without palm oil where possible, and really like the options that come in blocks rather than spreadable tubs.

Non-dairy cheese

Vegan cheese doesn't always get the best reputation, but there are some great options out there, so please find your favourite to use in our recipes.

Non-dairy cream

We love oat cream, and there are even 'whippable' options now if you want to add more thickness.

Meat alternatives

Vegan sausages

For all of our recipes using vegan sausages, the ones that will work best are those in a 'skin' that are super meaty. They provide a much better bite and flavour than vegetable-based sausages. If cooking a gluten-free recipe, ensure you choose gluten-free vegan sausage.

Vegan burgers

There is so much choice now when it comes to vegan burgers, simply use your favourite ones in any recipes calling for these. It cooking a gluten-free recipe, ensure you choose gluten-free vegan burgers.

Vegan 'chicken'

We usually use a soy-based 'chicken' and look for ones with really minimal ingredients and additives. If cooking a gluten-free recipe, ensure you choose gluten-free vegan 'chicken'. There are lots of good options in the frozen or chilled section in the supermarket.

Vegan 'bacon'

We love the streaky-style 'bacon', and use that option in most of our recipes. All good supermarkets will now stock a vegan 'bacon', so try a few and see which is your favourite. If cooking a gluten-free recipe, ensure you choose gluten-free vegan 'bacon'.

Vegan mince

This usually comes in either a drier, more crumbly form or one that almost identically replicates traditional minced beef. We prefer to use the latter, but find your preference. If cooking a gluten-free recipe, be sure to check the packaging to ensure the mince is gluten-free.

Pantry

Chickpea (gram) flour

This is an amazing gluten-free flour that also acts as a great binding agent. You will find this in the world food section of all good supermarkets.

Tapioca flour (starch)

This super stretchy flour has many applications. We primarily use it when making vegan cheese to add that amazing cheese-like elasticity.

Corn meal

This gluten free and high protein product is super versatile, especially in vegan burger patties. Adding a bit of bite and also acting as a great binder.

Nutritional yeast flakes

An absolute staple in any vegan's pantry and affectionately known as 'nooch'. Not only does this add an amazing nutty and cheesy flavour, it's also packed with B vitamins.

Black salt (kala namak)

One of our favourite discoveries for adding an egg-like flavour to recipes, such as our Dippy Egg and Soy-free Scrambled Egg. Use sparingly, it's potent stuff!

Vital wheat gluten

This is not an ingredient we use often, as we like to be as gluten-free-friendly as possible. However, it makes for an incredible flour substitute when you need a bit more bite and is packed with protein.

Aquafaba

This is simply the liquid you drain from a tin of chickpeas. However, you can also purchase it separately in supermarkets now. It whips to form an amazing egg white meringue consistency.

Chia seeds

These magical seeds turn gelatinous when combined with liquid and, again, make a great binder. They are also packed with nutrients, are high in fibre and high in omega 3.

Textured vegetable protein (TVP)

Textured vegetable protein is one of the oldest sources of vegan protein and is shelf stable; just mix with water and your favourite flavours to bring it to life. You can also get TVP in all sorts of shapes so it's super versatile.

Rice paper

Those magical sheets, used to make spring rolls, add an incredible crunch to many meat replacement options in the vegan world. Find it in the world foods section of most supermarkets.

Nori (dried seaweed)

Available in sheets or as a garnish for sprinkling, nori adds an incredible umami taste and depth of flavour reminiscent of the ocean to many plant-based dishes. It's a nutritional powerhouse, high in vitamins A, C and B12 plus iron, manganese and iodine.

Hearts of palm

This is a tinned vegetable product, and makes for a great seafood alternative. If you are struggling to get hold of this, the stems of king oyster mushrooms make for a great replacement.

Jackfruit

A tinned fruit product with a fibrous texture similar to meat, which is now readily available in most supermarkets. It needs to be drained and squeezed well to replicate that pulled meat-like texture.

Fridge

Black garlic

This is a type of aged garlic which adds a beautiful caramel/umami tone to dishes. We find it easier to buy this in paste format, as it keeps in the fridge for ages.

Vegan mayo

Makes an amazing egg replacer/ binder in many batters and even cake mixes, and gives a super light and fluffy texture. We would always recommend our very own Original Mayo. We also use our Smoky 'Bacon' Mayo in a couple of recipes, which we would also really recommend sourcing.

Miso paste

A traditional Japanese seasoning and very popular in vegan cooking. Super rich and salty, it adds a real 'meaty' flavour to dishes.

Puff pastry

Now we know this isn't a new ingredient, however, many people don't realise that most shop-bought pastry is accidentally vegan. Just watch out for 'all butter' varieties and always check the ingredients list.

Brunch

Brunch

'Bacon' 'n' Waffles

150g (5¼oz) self-raising flour or gluten-free self-raising flour

70g (2½oz) chickpea (gram) flour

1½ tsp baking powder

3 tbsp vegan mayo

300ml (10fl oz) vegan milk

To serve

8 rashers vegan 'bacon'

4 tbsp vegan butter

4 tbsp maple syrup

We don't want anyone to go without gorgeous fluffy waffles when they go vegan, and mayo makes for an amazing egg replacer in this recipe (trust us!). You can't go wrong with pairing waffles with sweet syrup and smoky vegan 'bacon', but feel free to add your favourite toppings.

1. In a mixing bowl, combine both the flours and the baking powder. Add the mayo and milk then whisk well until you have a smooth batter and no lumps remain. Place in the fridge to chill for about 20 minutes.

2. Preheat the waffle maker.

3. Ladle the batter into the hot waffle maker, close the lid and cook for 3–5 minutes until beautifully risen and fluffy. The batter mix should make about four decent-sized waffles.

4. Meanwhile, fry the 'bacon' until crispy.

5. Start stacking your waffles with the 'bacon' rashers, a tablespoon of butter and a tablespoon of maple syrup. Serve warm.

Caramelised Banana Bagel
with Blueberry Compote

For the blueberry compote

150g (5¼oz) frozen blueberries

3 tbsp caster sugar

For the caramelised bananas

2 tbsp brown sugar

½ tsp ground cinnamon

1 tbsp oil

2 bananas, cut diagonally into 2-cm (¾-inch) pieces

To serve

2 bagels or gluten-free bagels

3 tbsp almond butter

3 tbsp vegan yoghurt

30g (1oz) toasted coconut flakes

This recipe takes us back... we created this simple yet delicious dish in collaboration with Gaz Oakley back when Shoreditch first opened, and we would serve brunch on the weekends. A recipe that staff have continued to make over the years, even when the special had finished – so we couldn't not include it!

1. Make the blueberry compote by placing the blueberries and caster sugar in a small saucepan over a low heat. Stir frequently until the sugar has dissolved and the compote is gently bubbling. Keep an eye on the compote to make sure it doesn't burn and continue stirring until the blueberries and sugar thicken up slightly to form a glossy mixture.

2. Make the caramelised bananas by mixing the brown sugar and cinnamon together in a small bowl. Heat the oil in a frying pan over a medium heat and place the sliced bananas in the pan, cut side down. Sprinkle half the cinnamon sugar over the bananas and fry for 1–2 minutes.

3. Flip the banana slices over when the sugar starts to melt and sprinkle the remaining sugar over the top of the bananas. Fry for a further 2 minutes then flip them once more until the sugar is golden brown and caramelised on each side. Be careful not to burn the sugar.

4. Slice the bagels in half and toast them. Smooth almond butter over each toasted bagel half then spoon the warm blueberry compote evenly over the top, followed by the caramelised bananas. Finish with a dollop of yoghurt and a sprinkling of coconut flakes. Serve immediately.

SERVES 4–6

30 mins +20 mins

HIGH PROTEIN

GFO

Nutty Maple Granola

200g (7oz) oats or gluten-free oats

25g (1oz) hazelnuts, chopped

25g (1oz) walnuts, chopped

15g (½oz) sunflower seeds

½ tsp salt

½ tsp ground cinnamon

80g (2¾oz) coconut oil, melted

140g (5oz) maple syrup

1 tsp vanilla extract

To serve

vegan yoghurt

a handful of fresh raspberries

a drizzle of maple syrup

We wanted to create something incredibly simple that would give your breakfast a boost and was high in protein. Inspired by our Shoreditch brunch that we served back in 2018, the gorgeous toasted maple flavour of this granola is perfect served with your favourite vegan yoghurt and contains 10 grams of protein per serving.

1. Preheat the oven to 200°C fan/400°F/gas 7.

2. Place all the dry ingredients in a bowl and mix to combine. Add the coconut oil, maple syrup and vanilla extract and stir until fully incorporated.

3. Spoon the granola mixture onto a lined baking tray in an even layer and place in the preheated oven for 25 minutes.

4. Remove the granola from the oven and set aside to cool at room temperature for 30 minutes. You may need to break the bigger granola clusters into smaller pieces.

5. Store in an airtight container until ready to serve. It will keep for 7 days.

SERVES 8-10 · 15 mins · GFO

Perfect Pancakes

240g (8½oz) plain flour or gluten-free plain flour

1 tsp baking powder

3 tbsp sugar

½ tsp ground cinnamon

2 tbsp vegan mayo

1 tsp vanilla extract

350ml (12fl oz) vegan milk

4 tbsp oil, for frying

We know putting mayo in your pancakes sounds a bit strange, but you need to give these a go to believe it. It adds an element of airiness and makes these pancakes one of a kind. Simply serve with lemon and sugar, or one of our pancake toppers (see pages 29–31) for the ultimate breakfast.

1. In a large mixing bowl, combine the flour, baking powder, sugar and cinnamon. Add the mayo, vanilla extract and milk, then whisk well until you have a smooth batter and no lumps remain.

2. Melt a teaspoon of oil in a frying pan over a medium heat. When the oil is hot, ladle enough batter mix into the pan to make one pancake (use just under one ladleful for each pancake).

3. Cook until bubbles appear on the surface and the top of the pancake is no longer shiny. Flip the pancake over and cook on the other side for a further 2 minutes. Repeat until all of the batter mix has been used, adding a teaspoon of oil before cooking each pancake.

4. Cover the pancakes in foil and keep warm in a low oven while you cook the rest. Stack the pancakes on a serving plate and serve with your favourite toppings – we recommend our pancake toppers!

CHEF'S TIP: vegan mayo makes an amazing egg replacer in baking, hence why we use it in our batter recipes.

Pancake Toppers

SERVES 2 · 10 mins

Berry Biscoff

120g (4¼oz) mixed frozen berries

2 tbsp sugar

5 Biscoff biscuits, crushed

To serve

2 tbsp vanilla vegan yoghurt

I'm sure we aren't alone in saying that Biscoff holds a special place in our hearts, and together with the berries this slightly tart yet sweet speculoos flavour needs no further introduction.

1. Make a coulis by placing the frozen berries and sugar in a saucepan over a low heat. Cook gently, stirring continuously, for a few minutes until the berries have softened and the sugar has dissolved.

2. Drizzle the berry coulis over a perfect pancake and sprinkle some crushed Biscoff biscuits over the top. Repeat with the remaining pancakes, layering them into a stack.

3. Finish off the stack with the remaining compote, crushed Biscoff and a dollop of vanilla yoghurt.

Strawberry Whip

1½ tbsp aquafaba

½ tsp cream of tartar

3 tbsp strawberry jam

100ml (3½fl oz) vegan cream

To serve

a handful of fresh strawberries

Aquafaba is a magical ingredient, so make sure you are reserving the precious liquid when you drain a tin of chickpeas. It has both sweet and savoury applications, but if you whip it using an electric whisk with a little cream of tartar you get a mega fluffy whip that is just dreamy on a stack of pancakes.

1. Place the aquafaba and cream of tartar in a large clean mixing bowl and beat together using a hand-held electric whisk for about 5 minutes, until stiff peaks form.

2. Place the jam and cream in a separate bowl and beat together using the electric whisk.

3. Carefully fold the whipped aquafaba into the jam and cream mix; you are trying to keep as much air as possible in the mix for maximum fluffiness!

4. Place in the fridge to chill and firm up for at least 20 minutes.

5. Simply spoon onto your perfect pancakes and add a handful of fresh strawberries for the ultimate breakfast feast!

CHEF'S TIP: use whippable vegan cream to make the mixture extra thick and fluffy.

MAKES 250g (9oz) · 5 mins · GF

Chocolate Hazelnut Spread

80ml (2¾fl oz) vegetable oil

120g (4¼oz) hazelnuts, chopped

60g (2oz) maple syrup

2 tbsp cocoa powder

2 tbsp vegan milk

a pinch of salt

To serve

chopped hazelnuts

Inspired by the chocolate hazelnut milkshake in our restaurants, which is an absolute classic and loved by staff and customers alike. We wanted to create a quick and easy spread as an ode to this bestseller–try it yourself to believe the hype!

1. Place all the ingredients in a blender or food processor and blitz on high speed until smooth.

2. Smooth a layer of chocolate spread on top of your perfect pancakes and top with a sprinkling of extra chopped hazelnuts.

3. Any extra spread you have left over will keep in an airtight container in the fridge for about 2 weeks.

STRAWBERRY WHIP

CHOCOLATE
HAZELNUT SPREAD

MAKES 4 · 15 mins · GFO

French Toast Crumpets

80g (2¾oz) aquafaba

30g (1oz) chickpea (gram) flour

80g (2¾oz) maple syrup

40ml (1½fl oz) vegan cream

1 tsp ground cinnamon

2 tbsp oil

8 shop-bought crumpets or gluten-free crumpets

To serve

4 tbsp vegan butter

a handful of mixed fresh berries

4 tbsp maple syrup

Aquafaba is an amazing replacement for eggs, and paired with the gram flour this mixture can be used to turn your favourite carb into French toast. We are obsessed with crumpets and this sweet cinnamon mix is the perfect pairing.

1. Make the French toast mixture by placing the aquafaba in a clean mixing bowl and beating with a hand-held electric whisk until it becomes fluffy. Add the gram flour, maple syrup, cream and cinnamon, and whisk together until combined.

2. Melt the oil in a frying pan over a medium-low heat. Dip a crumpet into the French toast mixture, making sure it is fully coated on both sides.

3. When the oil is hot, place the crumpet in the pan and fry on each side for 2–3 minutes, until golden brown. Repeat with each crumpet and the remaining mixture. Cover the crumpets in foil and keep warm in a low oven while you cook the rest.

4. Stack the crumpets on a serving plate, top with the butter, fresh berries and maple syrup. Serve warm.

CHEF'S TIP: to make the mixture super light and fluffy, use a hand-held electric whisk to whip the aquafaba.

SERVES 4 | 40 mins | HIGH PROTEIN

Fully-loaded Breakfast Burrito
with 'Cheesy' Tofu Scramble

For the cheesy scramble

2 tbsp oil

1 shallot, finely chopped

150g (5¼oz) jarred red peppers, finely chopped

3 cloves garlic, minced

280g (10oz) firm tofu

1 tbsp smoked paprika

1 tbsp dried chives

2 tbsp tomato purée

3 tbsp nutritional yeast flakes

60ml (2fl oz) vegan milk

For the charred oyster mushrooms

400g (14oz) oyster mushrooms, brushed clean of visible debris

1 tbsp liquid smoke

To assemble

4 vegan sausages

4 large tortilla wraps

4 tbsp chilli jam

4 slices vegan cheese

a handful of spinach

4 tsp vegan mayo

Over years of developing many different brunch items for our menu, we really think that brunch can be in any format. Anything that starts with breakfast and ends in burrito is a winner in our eyes. This fully loaded option packs a protein punch too, with 27 grams per serving, so stack it high and wrap it up – feast to your heart's content!

1. Start by cooking the vegan sausages in a frying pan with a little oil. Once cooked, remove from the pan and set aside.

2. Make the cheesy scramble by adding a little more oil to the same pan and frying the shallot for a few minutes until translucent. Add the peppers and garlic, then crumble in the tofu. Add the paprika, chives and tomato purée and fry for a further 5 minutes until the tofu is golden. Finish by stirring through the nutritional yeast flakes and milk then remove from the heat, place in a bowl and set aside. Wipe out the frying pan with kitchen towels to use later.

3. To make the charred oyster mushrooms, place another frying pan over a medium-high heat. Once hot, add the mushrooms to the pan and place something heavy and heatproof on top of the mushrooms – this will help remove all the moisture and make sure they become charred and crispy. After about 2–3 minutes, flip the mushrooms over and repeat the weighing down process on the other side. Add the liquid smoke during the last minute of cooking, then remove from the heat and set aside.

4. Start to build the burritos by spreading a tablespoon of chilli jam in the middle of each wrap. Place a slice of cheese on top followed by a quarter of the spinach then add a quarter of the cheesy scramble mix to the bed of spinach. Slice each sausage in half lengthways and place two halved pieces onto each wrap, followed by a quarter of the charred mushrooms.

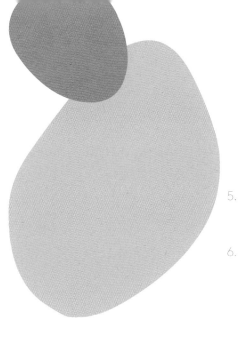

5. Finish by rolling each tortilla into a burrito shape, and just before sealing add a teaspoon of mayo to the outside edge of the wrap to ensure the seal sticks.

6. Heat a frying pan over a medium heat then place a burrito in the pan with the sealed edge facing down. Cook for 2–3 minutes until browned then flip over and cook for a further 2–3 minutes. Remove from the pan and wrap in foil then cut in half, on the diagonal, and serve while still warm.

CHEF'S TIP: use a heavy cast-iron pan to place on top of your mushrooms for the best, super crispy results.

Dippy 'Egg' & Soldiers

120ml (4fl oz) vegan milk

50ml (1¾fl oz) oil

a pinch of turmeric (this is just for colour, so add as much or as little as you like)

½ tsp onion powder

1 tbsp nutritional yeast flakes

1 tbsp cornflour

½ tsp black salt (kala namak)

To serve

4 slices buttered toast or gluten-free alternative

We are all about comforting eats, and nothing gets more nostalgic than a dippy egg and soldier. Serve in your favourite egg cup to relive your childhood comfort classics.

1. Pour the milk and oil into a saucepan and place it over a low heat. Add the turmeric, onion powder and nutritional yeast flakes and whisk to combine.

2. In a separate bowl, whisk the cornflour with 5 tablespoons of water. Add to the saucepan and continue whisking for a further minute until the mixture starts to thicken. When the mixture is glossy and has thickened slightly remove from the heat then stir in the black salt.

3. Spoon the dippy 'egg' mixture into a ramekin or egg cup and serve warm with toast.

CHEF'S TIP: black salt loses some of its flavour if heated too high so it's worth waiting until the end to add this and get the full 'egg' flavour.

SERVES 2–4 | 20 mins | HIGH PROTEIN | GFO

Soy-free Scrambled 'Egg'

180g (6¼oz) cooked yellow mung dal beans

1 tbsp nutritional yeast flakes

1 tsp garlic powder

1 tsp onion powder

1 tsp salt

30g cornflour

½ tsp turmeric

30ml (1fl oz) vegetable oil, plus 2 tbsp, for frying

200ml (7 fl oz) unsweetened vegan milk

60g (2oz) chickpea (gram) flour

½ tsp black pepper

½ tsp black salt (kala namak)

To serve

4 slices buttered toast or gluten-free alternative

a handful of fresh chopped chives

We are always partial to a tofu scramble, but wanted to create something that would really satisfy your egg cravings and also be soy free. This recipe is super high in protein, fibre and B vitamins too.

1. Place all the ingredients, except the black salt and 1 tablespoon of oil for frying in a high-speed blender and blitz until smooth.

2. Heat the 1 tablespoon of oil in a frying pan over a medium-low heat. Once hot, add half the blended 'egg' mixture to the pan and cook until the mixture starts to thicken. As the mixture starts to cook, stir it gently with a balloon whisk to make sure the mixture cooks evenly as it scrambles. This will take longer to cook than traditional scrambled eggs – about 15 minutes. Use the whisk to break up the scramble into smaller fluffy pieces. Once cooked, place in a bowl, cover and keep warm in a low oven then repeat to cook the remaining half of the mixture.

3. Once all the mixture is cooked, remove from the heat and add the black pepper and black salt, to taste.

4. Serve immediately on hot buttered toast, topped with the fresh chopped chives.

CHEF'S TIP: cooking this mixture in smaller batches will ensure it cooks more quickly and evenly.

SERVES 2 · **10 mins** · **GF**

Pea-vocado on Toast

500g (1.1lb) frozen peas

90ml (3fl oz) vegan cream

1 tsp salt

1 tsp pepper

juice of 1 lemon

To serve

4 slices of your favourite bread

a pinch of chilli flakes

a few lemon wedges

As we all try to be as environmentally conscious as possible, we wanted to try and replicate the millennial brunch classic of avocado on toast but with fewer food miles. Still creamy and delicious, our pea-vocado hits the spot and is also packed with goodness – it's naturally high in fibre, as well as folic acid and vitamins A and C.

1. Place the frozen peas in a saucepan and boil them according to the packet instructions. Once cooked, drain well and place in a mixing bowl. Add the cream, salt, pepper and lemon juice and lightly mash with a potato masher until the pea-vocado has a creamy, spread-like consistency.

2. Lightly toast the bread then spread a layer of pea-vocado over the top of each slice. Top with a pinch of chilli flakes and a lemon wedge on the side.

CHEF'S TIP: for an ultra-smooth consistency, use a stick blender instead of a potato masher.

SERVES 2 or 4 as a side | **30 mins** | **GF** | **HIGH PROTEIN**

Smoky Sausage & Potato Hash

with Lemon Aioli

For the hash

2 Maris Piper potatoes, cut into cubes

2 tbsp vegetable oil

1 red onion, diced

4 vegan sausages, sliced widthways into 1-cm (½-inch) rounds

1 tbsp smoked paprika

1 tbsp chipotle paste

a pinch of salt and pepper

a handful of spinach

5 sun-dried tomatoes, chopped

2 tbsp balsamic vinegar

2 tbsp tamari

a handful of chopped fresh chives

For the lemon aioli

2 tbsp vegan mayo

1 tbsp lemon juice

½ tsp salt

1 tsp garlic powder

1 tbsp nutritional yeast flakes

Sometimes you want a full English without the hassle of all the pots and pans, and this is exactly what this dish gives you. All the flavour, less hassle, and done in 30 minutes. And with 25 grams of protein per serving this hearty breakfast will set you up for the day ahead.

1. Bring a pan of salted water to the boil then add the cubed potato and boil for about 5 minutes, until fork tender.

2. Meanwhile, heat 1 tablespoon of the oil in a large frying pan over a medium heat, add the onion and fry for 3 minutes until slightly softened. Add the sliced sausages and fry for a further 7–8 minutes until they are cooked through and slightly browned. Add the smoked paprika and chipotle paste and a pinch of seasoning. Fry for a further 2 minutes, then remove the mixture from the pan and set aside.

3. Once cooked, drain the potatoes and either allow them to steam dry or pat them dry with kitchen towels. Add the remaining tablespoon of oil to the frying pan and place over a medium heat. Once hot, add the potatoes and fry for 8–10 minutes until golden on all sides and slightly crispy.

4. Add the sausage and onion mix to the potatoes in the pan. Add the remaining ingredients, reserving a few pinches of chives to use as a garnish. Mix to combine and fry for a further 2–3 minutes until the wet ingredients have been adsorbed.

5. Make the lemon aioli by mixing all the ingredients together in a bowl until combined.

6. Serve the potato hash on a warmed plate or straight from the pan, drizzle over the lemon aioli and garnish with the reserved chopped chives.

CHEF'S TIP: for extra crispy potatoes, you can pop these in the oven or air fryer to crisp up while the sausages are cooking. This is also an amazing way to use up leftover roast potatoes.

Sunshine Smoothie

1 ripe mango

2 passionfruits

100ml (3½fl oz) apple juice

2 tbsp hemp hearts

50g (1¾oz) oats or gluten-free oats

50g (1¾oz) vegan yoghurt

50ml (1¾fl oz) vegan milk

Inspired by our Mango Exotic Shake that we launched back in summer 2021, this protein-rich sunshine smoothie will put a smile on your face and a pep in your step, with 10 grams of protein per serving.

1. Roughly dice the mango, scoop the passionfruit pulp and place both in a blender. Add the remaining ingredients and blitz until smooth.

2. Pour into two glasses and enjoy.

CHEF'S TIP: add a scoop of your favourite vegan protein powder for a major protein boost.

Lighter Lunches

Lighter Lunches

SERVES 2 | 40 mins | GF | HIGH PROTEIN

East-side 'Meatball' Bowl

with Tofu 'Meatballs' and Edamame Crush

For the tofu 'meatballs'

125g (4½oz) firm tofu

1 spring onion, diced

1 clove garlic, diced

1 tbsp sriracha

1 tbsp tomato paste

1 tbsp tamari

1 tsp lemongrass paste

30g (1oz) chickpea (gram) flour

a small handful of chopped fresh coriander

a small handful of chopped fresh Thai basil

a pinch of salt

oil, for drizzling

For the edamame pea crush

60g (2oz) frozen edamame beans

50g (1¾oz) frozen peas

1 tbsp olive oil

1 tsp dried mint

½ tsp salt

½ tsp garlic powder

For the sesame dressing

2 tbsp sesame oil

1 tbsp almond butter

1 tsp red wine vinegar

1 tsp tamari

To serve

a bag of lamb's leaf lettuce

shredded carrot

crispy onions

toasted peanuts (optional)

One of our personal favourite collaborations with Gaz Oakley was our East-side Sub, launched back in 2019, which featured these gorgeous fresh tofu 'meatballs'. We've taken that recipe and turned it into this super light and filling bowl which is high in protein and packed with flavour.

1. Preheat the oven to 180°C fan/350°F/gas 6.

2. To make the tofu 'meatballs', squeeze the tofu to remove excess water. Don't worry if the tofu crumbles as you are squeezing, you are going to break it apart anyway.

3. Add all the tofu 'meatball' ingredients except the oil to a food processor and pulse until the mix comes together. Alternatively, add all the ingredients to a mixing bowl and lightly mash using a potato masher until everything is combined.

4. Form the mix into 15–20g (½oz) balls and place onto a baking tray lined with parchment paper. Drizzle with oil and bake in the preheated oven for 15 minutes, turning them halfway through the cooking time.

5. Make the edamame pea crush. Place the edamame beans and frozen peas in a saucepan and boil them according to the packet instructions. Once cooked, drain well and place in a mixing bowl with the remaining ingredients and mash together using a potato masher.

6. Place all the ingredients for the sesame dressing in a small bowl and whisk together.

7. Divide the lettuce between two bowls and place some shredded carrot on top. Add the tofu 'meatballs', followed by the edamame pea crush. Finish with crispy onions, toasted peanuts, if using, and the sesame dressing.

Hasselback Harissa Aubergine
with Crispy 'Pork' Mince & Basil Oil

For the hasselback aubergine

2 aubergines

1 tsp salt

400g (14oz) tomato passata

2 tbsp harissa paste

For the crispy 'pork' mince

3 tbsp vegetable oil

200g (7oz) vegan mince

2 tsp sweet smoked paprika

½ tsp garlic powder

½ tsp onion powder

½ tsp dried sage

½ tsp salt

¼ tsp chilli powder

For the basil oil

15g (½oz) fresh basil leaves

2 cloves garlic

50ml (1¾fl oz) olive oil

To serve

3 tbsp vegan yoghurt

a handful of salad leaves

fresh basil leaves

An ode to our longest standing menu item – the Auburger. We absolutely love how versatile aubergines are, they are such a good carrier for any flavour, with this smoky harissa pairing perfectly with crispy pork-style mince.

1. Preheat the oven to 200°C fan/400°F/gas 7.

2. To make the hasselback aubergine, make slits about 1cm (½ inch) thick lengthways through the aubergines, cutting through the whole aubergine but leaving about 2–3cm (1 inch) uncut at the top stem. Spread both the aubergines out into a fan shape and sprinkle the exposed aubergine flesh well with the salt.

3. Place the passata and harissa paste in a deep baking tray and mix together. Place the aubergines on top of the tomato harissa mixture and spoon a few tablespoons of the mixture between the slices of aubergine flesh.

4. Bake in the preheated oven for 30 minutes.

5. To make the crispy 'pork' mince, heat the oil in a frying pan over a high heat. Once hot, add the mince and break it up with a wooden spoon as it fries. Add the spices and fry for about 8–10 minutes until the mince is a deep golden brown and crispy.

6. Place all the ingredients for the basil oil in a mortar and grind with a pestle until you have a silky green oil, or place the ingredients in a beaker that can accommodate a stick blender and blitz until everything comes together.

7. Once cooked, remove from the oven and place the aubergines on a plate, spooning over as much of the tomato harissa sauce as you like. Sprinkle the crispy mince over the top, then garnish with the basil oil, some yoghurt, salad and basil leaves.

CHEF'S TIP: broken up vegan sausage meat also works really well if you don't have vegan mince to hand.

SERVES 2–4 | 60 mins | HIGH PROTEIN

Black Garlic Flatbreads
with Umami Onions & Sticky Balsamic Sausages

Umami is one of those food trends that comes up for us time and time again, and we totally know why! The pairing of fluffy homemade flatbreads with sweet umami onions and sticky sausages is a marriage of flavours we are obsessed with.

For the flatbreads

1 tsp instant yeast
60ml (2fl oz) warm water
320g (11¼oz) self-raising flour
½ tsp salt
235g (8¼oz) plain vegan yoghurt

For the umami onions

2 tbsp vegetable oil
3 red onions, finely sliced
1 tbsp soy sauce
1 tbsp brown sugar
1 tsp liquid smoke
a pinch each of salt and pepper

For the sticky balsamic sausages

6 vegan sausages
2 tbsp vegetable oil
4 tbsp balsamic vinegar

To serve

4 tbsp black garlic paste
a handful of rocket
vegan feta, crumbled

1. Start by preparing the flatbreads. Mix the yeast and warm water together in a mixing bowl and set aside for about 10 minutes until bubbly. Once the yeast has been activated, sift the flour into the mixing bowl then add the salt and yoghurt. Mix well and knead lightly for 5 minutes until you have a smooth and elastic dough. Cover with a clean tea towel and leave in a warm place to rise for 30 minutes.

2. Meanwhile, make the umami onions. Heat the oil in a frying pan over a medium heat then add the sliced onions with a pinch of salt. Let the onions sweat down and soften, stirring frequently, for about 20 minutes. Add the soy sauce, brown sugar and liquid smoke and cook over a low heat for a further 20 minutes to continue caramelising.

3. Cut the sausages on the diagonal into 1-cm (½-inch) thick slices. Heat some oil in a frying pan and cook the sausages until they are golden. Add the balsamic vinegar and cook for 5 minutes until they are fully coated and sticky. Remove from the heat and set aside.

4. Once the flatbread dough has risen, preheat a clean frying pan or skillet over a high heat. Divide the dough into quarters and lightly dust a clean work surface with flour. Use a rolling pin to roll out each piece of dough into an oval 1cm (½ inch) thick then place in the hot pan. Cook each flatbread for 4 minutes on each side; air bubbles will form as they cook and the flatbreads will turn golden and char in places. Keep the flatbreads warm in a low oven until ready to serve.

5. Spread the black garlic paste evenly over the flatbreads. Add a handful of rocket then the balsamic sausages, umami onions and finish by crumbling over some feta.

CHEF'S TIP: if you are struggling to get hold of black garlic paste, hummus will make a great substitute here.

SERVES 2 | 30 mins | GFO | HIGH PROTEIN

Ultimate Caesar Salad
with Herby Sourdough Croutons

As well as providing people with feel-good fast food since 2016, we have also wanted to provide incredible salads that don't leave you feeling like you've missed out. This Caesar salad is an adaptation of the one on our main menu, and it hits every spot. Truly satisfying and deliciously moreish – a real staple.

For the Caesar dressing

140g (5oz) vegan mayo

20g (¾oz) gherkins, diced

2 tbsp nutritional yeast flakes

1 tsp vegan Worcestershire sauce

1 tsp Dijon mustard

½ tsp garlic powder

1 tbsp lemon juice

a pinch of black pepper

For the herby sourdough croutons

200g (7oz) sourdough or gluten-free bread, cut into 2.5-cm (1-inch) cubes

4 tbsp olive oil

1 tsp dried mixed herbs

1 tsp garlic powder

½ tsp salt

½ tsp black pepper

To serve

200g (7oz) vegan 'chicken' pieces

100g (3½oz) vegan 'bacon' lardons

2 small heads romaine lettuce, shredded

2 large tomatoes, diced

2 tbsp vegan Parmesan

1. Preheat the oven to 180°C fan/350°F/gas 6.

2. Start by preparing the croutons. Place the sourdough cubes on a baking sheet lined with parchment paper. Drizzle over the oil, mixed herbs, garlic powder, salt and pepper, and mix until the bread is fully coated. Bake in the preheated oven for 15 minutes, then remove from the oven and set aside to cool until ready to serve.

3. Place all the dressing ingredients in a bowl, mix well to combine then place in the fridge to chill.

4. Meanwhile, cook the 'chicken' pieces and 'bacon' lardons according to the packet instructions and season to taste.

5. Assemble the salad by dividing the lettuce and tomato between two plates. Layer the 'chicken' pieces and 'bacon' lardons evenly over the top. Drizzle over the Caesar dressing, top with a handful of the herby sourdough croutons and finish with a sprinkling of the vegan Parmesan.

SERVES 2 · 20 mins · HIGH PROTEIN · GF

Sticky BBQ Lettuce Cups

For the sticky tempeh filling

1 tbsp tamari
1 tbsp sriracha
1 tsp maple syrup
250g (9oz) tempeh, cubed
2 tbsp oil
1 red onion, roughly chopped
1 red pepper, roughly chopped
3 cloves garlic, minced

For the BBQ sauce

50g (1¾oz) tomato passata
1 tsp tomato purée
1½ tsp brown sugar
½ tsp onion powder
½ tsp garlic powder
¼ tsp black pepper
½ tsp salt
¼ tsp ground coriander
¼ tsp ground cumin
1 tbsp tamari
1 ½ tsp yellow mustard
1 tsp agave syrup
2 tsp liquid smoke
1 tsp cider vinegar

To serve

1 head butter lettuce
a handful of flaked almonds

An ode to our hickory BBQ sauce, and also to tempeh, which has been a key component of the veg-based patties in our restaurants. Sometimes you want something fresh and light but something that is still packed with flavour, and this ticks all the boxes.

1. Prepare a marinade for the tempeh by placing the soy sauce, sriracha and maple syrup in a shallow bowl and mixing well to combine. Add the tempeh and spoon over the marinade, making sure it is fully coated, and set aside to marinate.

2. Make the BBQ sauce by placing all the ingredients in a pan over a low heat. Stir to combine and simmer for 10 minutes, stirring occasionally until the sauce has thickened slightly.

3. While the sauce is simmering prepare the filling. Heat half the oil in a frying pan over a medium heat, add the onion and red pepper and sauté for 5 minutes until softened. Push the onions and peppers to the side of the pan and add the remaining tablespoon of oil. Add the marinated tempeh and fry for 5–7 minutes, turning it regularly to make sure each side turns golden brown. In the last minute of cooking add the minced garlic and stir to bring everything together. Add the BBQ sauce and mix through.

4. Wash and dry the lettuce, keeping each leaf whole, and divide the leaves between two plates. Spread the tempeh mixture evenly over each lettuce leaf, top with the flaked almonds and extra BBQ sauce to taste.

CHEF'S TIP: double or even triple the BBQ sauce recipe and store in the fridge for up to 4 weeks.

Ultimate Salad Boosters

SERVES 4 · 25 mins · GF · HIGH PROTEIN

Protein Trail Mix

400g (14oz) tin chickpeas
1 tbsp vegetable oil
1 tbsp nutritional yeast flakes
½ tsp dried sage
½ tsp dried basil
½ tsp dried oregano
½ tsp salt
½ tsp pepper
½ tsp onion powder
½ tsp garlic powder
70g (2½oz) walnuts, roughly chopped
40g (1½oz) flaked almonds
3 tbsp hemp seeds
45g (1½oz) pumpkin seeds
15g (½oz) fresh basil leaves
zest of 1 lemon

A delicious way to add texture and crunch to any salad, as well as boosting the nutritionals with 15g of protein per serving.

1. Preheat the oven to 200°C fan/400°F/gas 7.

2. Drain the chickpeas, reserving the aquafaba for another recipe, and rinse until the water runs clear. Pat the chickpeas dry and place on a baking tray lined with parchment paper. Add the oil, nutritional yeast flakes, dried herbs and seasonings and mix well to fully coat the chickpeas. Bake in the preheated oven for 15 minutes.

3. Meanwhile, mix the walnuts, almonds, hemp and pumpkin seeds together in a bowl and set aside. Chop the fresh basil leaves very finely, until almost a mince.

4. After the chickpeas have been roasting for 15 minutes, remove the baking tray from the oven, add the nut and seed mix and toss everything together. Return to the oven for a further 5 minutes then remove and set aside to cool slightly.

5. Finally, add the basil and lemon zest and mix to combine.

6. Store in an airtight storage container in the fridge for up to 3 days.

Coconut 'Bacon'

SERVES 6 · 25 mins · GF

We have been making this recipe since the very beginnings of The Vurger Co. so we had to include it. Add this to your burgers too for the ultimate smoky crunch.

120g (4¼oz) coconut flakes

1 tbsp oil

1 tbsp maple syrup

2 tbsp tamari

½ tsp smoked paprika

½ tsp liquid smoke

½ tsp salt

1. Preheat the oven to 150°C fan/300°F/gas 3½.

2. Place all the ingredients in a mixing bowl and stir gently to combine, taking care not to break up the coconut flakes. Place on a baking tray lined with parchment paper and bake in the preheated oven for 5 minutes.

3. After the coconut flakes have been roasting for 5 minutes, remove the baking tray from the oven and give everything another good mix to make sure nothing catches. Return to the oven for a further 5 minutes then remove and set aside to cool. The flakes should be a deep golden brown colour, so give them a few minutes more or less in the oven as necessary.

4. Store in an airtight storage container for up to 7 days.

CHEF'S TIP: these will firm up and go crispy once cool.

Cashew Parm

SERVES 10 · 5 mins · GF · HIGH PROTEIN

1. Place all the ingredients in a blender or food processor and pulse until a fine crumb forms.

2. Store in an airtight storage container for up to 2 weeks.

CHEF'S TIP: this versatile topping gives any pasta dish a boost too!

100g (3½oz) cashews

3 tbsp nutritional yeast flakes

½ tsp salt

½ tsp garlic powder

COCONUT 'BACON'

PROTEIN TRAIL MIX

CASHEW
PARM

SERVES 2 • 30 mins • GFO

Teriyaki 'Duck' Bowl

For the sticky broccoli

220g (8oz) Tenderstem broccoli

1 tbsp vegetable oil

1 tbsp soy sauce or tamari

1 tbsp maple syrup

1 tsp chilli flakes

For the teriyaki sauce

a thumb-sized piece of ginger, minced

50g (1¾oz) light brown sugar

100ml (3½oz) soy sauce or tamari

2 tbsp mirin

1 tbsp sesame oil

1½ tsp garlic powder

1 tbsp rice wine vinegar

80ml (2¾fl oz) orange juice

1 tbsp cornflour

For the crispy 'duck'

220ml (7½fl oz) vegetable oil, for frying

3 tbsp cornflour

1 tsp five spice

8 large oyster mushrooms (about 200g/7oz), cleaned and cut into strips

To serve

1 bag baby leaf salad

½ cucumber, ribboned

1 large orange, sliced

a handful of spring onions, sliced

1 tbsp sesame seeds

Inspired by our super popular teriyaki special back in 2019, this sticky umami sauce is perfect paired with vegan 'duck'. Oyster mushrooms make the perfect duck replica, but if you want a quicker prep time you can simply swap this out for a vegan duck replacement.

1. Preheat the oven to 180°C fan/350°F/gas 6.

2. Start by making the sticky broccoli. Place the Tenderstem on a baking tray lined with parchment paper, drizzle over the remaining liquid ingredients and sprinkle over the chilli flakes. Place in the preheated oven for 14–16 minutes. Keep an eye on it – it will catch easily.

3. To prepare the teriyaki sauce, heat a little oil in a saucepan over a medium heat. Add the minced ginger and fry for 2 minutes then add the brown sugar, stirring constantly until the sugar has dissolved. Add the soy sauce, mirin, sesame oil, garlic powder and vinegar and stir thoroughly, then leave to simmer over a low heat.

4. In a measuring jug mix together 80ml (2¾fl oz) water with the orange juice and cornflour. When the teriyaki sauce is boiling, add the cornflour mix to the pan and stir. Reduce to a simmer and stir until the mixture thickens, this should take about 5 minutes.

5. To make the crispy 'duck', heat the oil in a deep-sided frying pan over a medium heat. Combine the cornflour and five spice in a small bowl then add the mushroom strips, gently tossing them in the cornflour until fully coated. Fry the strips for 2 minutes, or until golden and crispy. Place on a plate lined with kitchen towel to remove excess oil or remove from the pan using a slotted spoon.

6. Divide the lettuce between two bowls and layer the cucumber ribbons and orange slices on top. Add the sticky broccoli, crispy 'duck' and spoon over the teriyaki sauce. Finish with the spring onions and sesame seeds.

SERVES 3-4 · 30 mins · GFO

For the fritters

½ head of cauliflower, cut into florets

2 tbsp sesame oil

5 spring onions, trimmed

1 tsp sea salt

a handful of finely chopped fresh coriander

zest and juice of 1 lime

200g (7oz) frozen spinach

250ml (9fl oz) vegan milk

180g (6¼oz) self-raising flour or gluten-free self-raising flour

2 tbsp sesame seeds

3 tbsp chia seeds

2 cloves garlic, minced

1 chilli, finely chopped

olive oil, for frying

salt and pepper, to taste

For the sweet chilli sauce

125ml (4¼fl oz) white wine vinegar

100g (3½oz) caster sugar

2–4 tbsp dried chilli flakes (depending on how spicy you want it)

a thumb-sized piece of ginger, minced

1 tsp sea salt

2 tbsp cornflour

To serve

mixed salad leaves

1 lime, cut into wedges

Charred Cauliflower Fritters

A RECIPE BY CHEF GAZ OAKLEY

Charring the cauliflower really gives a depth of flavour and brings these fritters to life. The batter is great to make in advance and keep in the fridge ready for a quick lunch; it will keep for up to 3 days. The sweet chilli sauce can be stored in the fridge in an airtight storage container for up to a month.

1. To prepare the cauliflower, steam the florets in a steamer or a pan filled with boiling water and a steaming basket for 3–4 minutes, or until tender. Heat the sesame oil on a griddle pan over a high heat then add the steamed cauliflower and spring onions and griddle them for 4–5 minutes, or until they are lightly charred. Transfer to a chopping board and cut into small pieces.

2. Place the cauliflower and spring onions in a large mixing bowl, add the salt, coriander, lime zest and juice and mix. Add the remaining fritter ingredients except the olive oil and mix well to combine.

3. Heat a little olive oil in a large non-stick frying pan over a medium heat then spoon a couple of tablespoons of the batter into the pan. Use the back of the spoon to form the batter into a rough disc shape. Fry the fritters in batches of three, frying each fritter for 4–5 minutes on each side. They should fluff up as they cook and more or less double in thickness. Once the fritters are golden, transfer to a plate and keep warm in a low oven while you cook the remainder and all the batter has been used.

4. Place all the ingredients for the sweet chilli sauce, except the cornflour, in a small saucepan over a low-medium heat. Bring to a simmer, stirring, until the sugar has melted. Mix the cornflour with a splash of water to form a loose paste and whisk it into the sauce until it has thickened, then turn off the heat.

5. Serve the fritters on a plate with a side salad of mixed leaves, lime wedges and the sweet chilli sauce.

CHEF'S TIP: start with less chilli flakes in the sweet chilli sauce and add more to taste; some varieties are much spicier than others.

Crunchy Taco Bowl
with Spiced Fajita Strips & Lime Crema

For the fajita spice mix

1 tbsp ground cumin

1 tbsp paprika

1 tsp garlic powder

1 tsp ground coriander

1 tsp onion powder

1 tsp salt

½ tsp black pepper

½ tsp chilli powder

For the fajita pieces

50g (1¾oz) textured vegetable protein (TVP)

100ml (3½floz) vegetable stock

1 tbsp vegetable oil

1 tbsp tomato purée

1 tbsp hot sauce

1 tbsp liquid smoke

For the spiced rice

1 tbsp vegetable oil

1 red onion, diced

4 garlic cloves, minced

30g (1oz) jarred jalapeños, roughly chopped

1 tsp smoked paprika

1 tsp ground cumin

1 tsp ground coriander

½ tsp chilli powder

250g (9oz) cooked basmati rice

200g (7oz) tinned black beans, drained weight

We wanted to spice up taco Tuesday by turning your classic tacos into an edible bowl filled with spiced goodness. You can use any vegan protein here but we love how TVP absorbs flavours and its versatility.

1. Place all the ingredients for the spice mix in a mixing bowl, stir to combine and set aside in an airtight storage container.

2. Place the TVP in a mixing bowl, add a tablespoon of the spice mix and pour over the hot stock. Set aside for 5 minutes to allow the TVP to fully rehydrate.

3. Heat the oil in a frying pan over a medium heat, then add the TVP and a further tablespoon of the spice mix. Fry for 1 minute, then add the tomato purée, hot sauce and liquid smoke. Lower the heat and fry for a further 2 minutes, then tip into a bowl and set aside.

4. Wipe out the frying pan ready to make the spiced rice, pour in the oil and place it back over the heat. Add the onion, garlic and jalapeños and fry until the onion becomes slightly translucent, then add the spices. Gradually add the rice, stirring continuously, then the black beans. Cook for a further 5 minutes then set aside.

5. To make the lime crema, measure out 100ml (3½fl oz) of the hardened coconut cream and 100ml (3½fl oz) of the coconut water. Place the coconut cream and water in a mixing bowl, add the lime juice, coriander and salt, and mix thoroughly – it should have a yoghurt-like consistency. If it is a little too thick add some more coconut water to thin it down. Place in the fridge until needed.

6. Preheat the oven to 200°C fan/400°F/gas 7.

For the lime crema

200ml (7fl oz) coconut milk, refrigerated to separate the cream and the water

juice of 1 lime

a handful of chopped fresh coriander

½ tsp salt

For the tortilla bowls

2 large tortilla wraps

1 tbsp vegetable oil

To serve

shredded lettuce

40g (1½oz) vegan cheese, grated

50g (1¾oz) tomato salsa

fresh jalapeños (optional)

fresh coriander (optional)

7. Make the tortilla bowls by brushing both sides of each tortilla with the oil. Invert two heatproof bowls and drape the tortillas over the base of the bowls, gently shaping them to follow the shape of the bowls. Place another heatproof bowl that is the same size and shape over each tortilla to press it into shape, so the tortillas are sandwiched between the two bowls. Place the bowls in the preheated oven and cook for 10 minutes, then remove from the oven and lift off the top bowls so the tortillas are exposed. Bake for a further 5 minutes to crisp up the bottom of each bowl. Remove from the oven and leave to cool, keeping the bowl underneath the tortilla for at least 5 minutes when the tortilla bowl should then be able to hold its shape.

8. Line the tortilla bowl with shredded lettuce, then spoon some spiced rice on top. Add the fajita pieces, along with some grated cheese and tomato salsa. Finish with a drizzle of the lime crema, fresh coriander and jalapenos, if using.

CHEF'S TIP: try and choose a coconut milk with minimal ingredients and stabilisers, otherwise it won't separate in the fridge.

SERVES 4–6 · 15 mins · GFO

15-minute Tortilla Pizza

A RECIPE BY CHEF GAZ OAKLEY

For the base

4–6 large wheat tortillas or gluten-free alternative

For the pizza sauce

225g (8oz) tomato purée

1 tbsp sugar

1 tbsp garlic granules/powder

2 tbsp dried mixed herbs

1 tbsp balsamic vinegar

3 tbsp extra virgin olive oil, plus extra for drizzling

1 tsp sea salt

For the toppings

1 courgette, cut finely lengthways into ribbons

1 tomato, finely sliced

a handful of chestnut mushrooms, cleaned and finely sliced

85g (3oz) vegan mozzarella cheese, grated

a pinch of chilli flakes

To serve

vegan pesto (optional)

a handful of fresh basil leaves

a handful of rocket (optional)

These super easy tortilla pizzas couldn't be simpler to make, and you can customise them with any of your favourite toppings.

1. Preheat the oven to 180°C fan/350°F/gas 6.

2. To make the pizza sauce, mix all the sauce ingredients together in a mixing bowl until fully incorporated.

3. Spread the pizza sauce generously over each tortilla, leaving a 1-cm (½-inch) border around the edge – this will become golden and crispy when cooked.

4. Top each pizza with your choice of toppings then season with salt, pepper and a small drizzle of olive oil.

5. Place each pizza on a baking sheet and cook them individually in the preheated oven for 8–10 minutes.

6. Remove from the oven and garnish with a drizzle of pesto, if using, fresh basil and rocket, if using.

Fakeaway

Fakeaway

How to build the perfect Vurger from top to bottom

The sauce: a winning sauce on the top and bottom bun will bring a lot of flavour to each bite. Sometimes we add another sauce on top of the patty if it needs a bit more moisture and another flavour dimension.

The cheese: not essential but a really great add on. You can get all sorts of sliced vegan cheeses now, from pepperjack to smoked gouda.

The patty: whether it's a chicken-style, beef-style, or vegetable based. Choose something that has a good bite and holds together well.

MLT
with Sun-dried Tomato Pesto

For the MLT patty

200g (7oz) button mushrooms, cleaned
2 tbsp soy sauce
240g (8½oz) tinned borlotti beans, drained weight
1 tbsp dried parsley
1 tsp salt
½ tbsp Marmite
40g (1½oz) breadcrumbs
50g (1¾oz) plain flour
oil, for frying

For the sun-dried tomato pesto

150g (5¼oz) sun-dried tomatoes in oil
30g (1oz) walnuts
1 tbsp nutritional yeast flakes
a handful of fresh basil

Back to where it all began... the MLT (mushroom, lettuce, tomato) was one of our most popular plant-based patties when we first opened our Shoreditch branch in 2018. We wanted to include it here and show people that plant-based patties can still be super delicious as well as nutritious. Best served with our Perfect Fries (see page 116).

1. Preheat the oven to 200°C fan/400°F/gas 7.

2. Place the mushrooms on a baking tray and drizzle over the soy sauce. Roast in the preheated oven for 15–20 minutes.

3. Meanwhile, place half the borlotti beans in a food processor and pulse to break them down. Place in a mixing bowl with the remainder of the beans – this will ensure the patties maintain some texture. Add the parsley, salt and Marmite and mix to combine.

4. Remove the mushrooms from the oven and set aside to cool, then place in a food processor and pulse until the mushrooms are a mince-like consistency. Add the mushrooms to the bowl and mix thoroughly, then add the breadcrumbs and flour, mixing until you have a slightly sticky, dough-like consistency.

5. To make the sun-dried tomato pesto, place all the ingredients in a food processor and pulse until everything comes together. If the pesto is a bit too dry you can add a little of the oil from the jar of sun-dried tomatoes to help the mixture blitz together.

6. To form the patties, divide the patty mixture into four equal parts and roll each in the palm of your hands to form a ball. Gently push down the ball using your hands or the bottom of a glass to form four burger patties.

To serve

4 slices vegan mozzarella

4 vegan brioche buns

4 tbsp burger sauce (see page 180)

4 lettuce leaves

sliced gherkins

7. Heat a teaspoon of oil in a non-stick frying pan over a medium heat and fry each patty for 2 minutes on each side until cooked through. Keep flipping the patty to make sure it doesn't burn on one side. During the last minute of cooking time, add a cheese slice to the top of each patty and place under the grill for 1 minute to melt.

8. To assemble the burger, lightly toast the brioche bun, spread the burger sauce on the bottom bun then add the lettuce leaf. Place the patty on top of the lettuce then add a quarter of the sun-dried tomato pesto to each burger. Finish with gherkins and a little more burger sauce then place the top bun over the top, securing it in place with a burger skewer to serve.

MLT history

The MLT (mushroom, lettuce, tomato) was one of our most popular plant-based patties when we first opened our Shoreditch branch in 2018.

Can you believe that we even get requests to this day to bring it back?

The MLT was originally made with Chef Andrew Dargue in our little kitchen in Stratford, East London.

We worked together on deepening the umami flavours and accentuating the saltiness with the gorgeous red pesto and rocket for crunch. The burger really elevated our menu, pioneering the mushroom burger from many outlets just providing a flat mushroom in a bun, to actually providing flavour and gorgeous texture.

We wanted to include it in this book, with slight tweaks to show everyone that plant-based patties can still be super delicious as well as super nutritious too. This is one recipe for all the family! We hope that everyone who has requested it from us over the years finds as much joy out of making this at home as we have serving it over the years.

Chipotle Corn Vurger
with Crispy Fried Jackfruit

SERVES 4 | **45 mins** | **GFO**

For the patties

80g (2¾oz) roasted red peppers

190g (6¾oz) tinned sweetcorn, drained weight

1 small red onion, finely chopped

2 tsp chipotle paste

3 cloves garlic, minced

1½ tsp smoked paprika

160g (5½oz) tinned butter beans, drained weight

35g (1¼oz) breadcrumbs or gluten-free alternative

35g (1¼oz) cornmeal

20g (¾oz) plain flour

12g (½oz) jarred jalapeños, finely chopped

½ tsp salt

½ tsp black pepper

For the crispy jackfruit

400g (14oz) tin jackfruit

2 tbsp rice flour

1 tbsp smoked paprika

½ tsp dried oregano

½ tsp cayenne pepper

½ tsp dried thyme

½ tsp sea salt

250ml (9fl oz) vegetable oil, for shallow frying

One of our first collaborations with Gaz Oakley, this beautiful fusion of spicy Mexican inspired flavours featured as a special in our Shoreditch restaurant back in 2019. The spicy corn fritter patty is beautiful paired with your favourite spicy mayo and the crispy spicy jackfruit – simply addictive!

1. Preheat the oven to 200°C fan/400°F/gas 7.

2. Place the red pepper, sweetcorn and red onion on a baking tray lined with parchment paper and roast in the preheated oven for 15 minutes. After 15 minutes, add the chipotle paste, minced garlic and paprika and mix through. Return to the oven for a further 5 minutes, then remove and set aside to cool.

3. Meanwhile, place the butter beans in a mixing bowl and roughly mash using a potato masher, leaving some beans whole to add texture.

4. Once cooled, add the cooked mixture from the baking tray and mix again. Add the breadcrumbs, cornmeal, flour, jalapeños and seasonings and mix.

5. To form the patties, divide the patty mixture into four equal parts and roll each in the palm of your hands to form a ball. Gently push down the ball using your hands or the bottom of a glass to form four burger patties. Place the patties in the fridge for 40 minutes to firm up.

6. Meanwhile, make the crispy jackfruit. Drain the liquid from the tin of jackfruit, place the jackfruit into a nut-milk bag or clean tea towel and twist and squeeze to expel as much water as you can. Once it's dry, place it in a mixing bowl with the remaining ingredients, except the oil, and mix thoroughly so the jackfruit is coated in all of the spices.

For the quick tomato salsa

10 cherry tomatoes, finely diced

a handful of chopped fresh coriander

½ red onion, finely diced

1 tbsp white wine vinegar

juice of ½ lime

½ tsp salt

To serve

4 slices vegan mozzarella

4 vegan brioche buns or gluten-free alternative

4 tbsp spicy vegan mayo

4 lettuce leaves

7. Heat the oil in a frying pan set over a medium-high heat. Fry the jackfruit in the hot oil, breaking it apart with a spoon to ensure the mix fries evenly. Fry for 3–4 minutes until evenly golden brown and crispy. Place on a plate lined with kitchen towel to remove any excess oil. Pour off all but 1 tablespoon of the oil from the frying pan, ready to fry the patties later.

8. To make the salsa, combine all the ingredients in a bowl and set aside until ready to serve.

9. Set the frying pan with the oil over a medium heat and fry the patties for 3 minutes on each side until cooked through. Keep flipping the patties to make sure they don't burn on one side. During the last minute of cooking time, add a cheese slice to the top of each patty and place under the grill for 1 minute to melt.

10. To assemble the burger, lightly toast the brioche bun. Spread the spicy mayo on the bottom bun then add the lettuce leaf. Place the patty on top of the lettuce then add the tomato salsa and jackfruit on top. Finish with a little more mayo then place the top bun over the top, securing it in place with a burger skewer to serve.

CHEF'S TIP: roasting the corn and peppers helps dry the ingredients out for a firmer patty, and also to caramelise the corn for more depth of flavour.

Chipotle Corn history

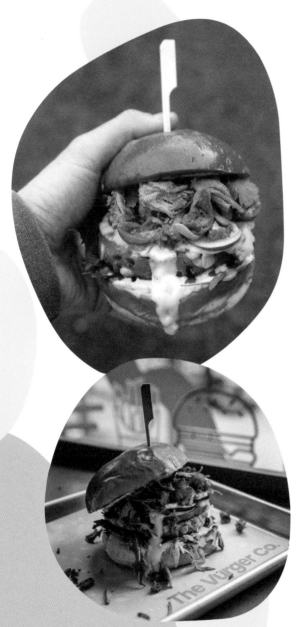

Created for us by Gaz Oakley in 2019 for our Shoreditch restaurant's first birthday, this festival of flavours brought us all so much joy!

We extended this special time and time again because it was so popular. Our original menu special featured a spicy corn fritter patty, crispy jackfruit pieces, tomato salsa, chilli mayo and a hot queso sauce.

The fusion of the sweet yet charred patty, with the super crispy spiced jackfruit and then the hot cheese queso was unmatched. The vegan burger scene was starting to gain a bit more traction, so each new menu item made us stand out from the competition more and more.

Every single element of this burger was made from scratch and we were incredibly proud of the hard work and love that our teams put into it. This burger became a staple for our Shoreditch branch, people were obsessed with all of the beautiful flavours that made it so unique to us. Here we spill all the secrets on how to make the beautiful crispy jackfruit pieces, and an upgraded recipe of the patty itself. We really hope you love it as much as we do.

SERVES 4 30 mins +30 mins HIGH PROTEIN

Meaty Smash Patties
with Asian-style Slaw

For the patties

90g (3¼oz) textured vegetable protein (TVP)
210ml (7fl oz) vegetable stock
5 cloves garlic, minced
a thumb-sized piece of ginger, chopped
2 spring onions, finely chopped
1 ½ tbsp soy sauce
1 tbsp Marmite
1 tbsp nutritional yeast flakes
½ tbsp apple cider vinegar
1 tsp onion powder
1 tsp dried mixed herbs
½ tsp black pepper
½ tsp Dijon mustard
50g (1¾oz) plain flour
80g (2¾oz) vital wheat gluten
40g (1½oz) coconut oil, chilled

These patties featured in our Teriyaki Special towards the end of 2020, and we had such amazing feedback on their texture that we had to include an adapted version in this book. Pair these patties with umami flavours, and any of your other favourite burger toppings.

1. Place the TVP in a mixing bowl and pour over the hot stock. Cover and set aside for 10 minutes to allow the TVP to rehydrate. When fully rehydrated, squeeze out any excess water that remains and place in a mixing bowl. Add all the remaining patty ingredients except the vital wheat gluten and coconut oil and mix to combine. Add the vital wheat gluten and mix everything together using your hands.

2. Knead the mixture for 5 minutes to fully form those gluten bonds, then add the coconut oil and press it into the mixture – the aim is for the oil to stay in small pockets throughout the mixture to add moisture.

3. To form the patties, divide the patty mixture into eight equal parts and roll each in the palm of your hands to form a ball. Gently push down the ball using your hands or the bottom of a glass to form eight burger patties. Place in between two sheets of parchment paper to press down further if necessary then stack up the patties on the parchment paper. Place in the fridge to chill for 30 minutes to firm up.

4. To make the slaw, place all the ingredients in a mixing bowl and stir until everything is evenly coated. Place in the fridge until needed.

5. To cook the patties, heat a teaspoon of oil in a non-stick frying pan over a medium heat and fry each patty for 2 minutes on each side until cooked through. Keep flipping the patties to make sure they don't burn on one side. During the last minute of cooking time, add a cheese slice to the top of each patty and place under the grill for 1 minute to melt.

For the Asian-style slaw

1 carrot, peeled and grated	
½ cucumber, peeled and grated	
½ red onion, finely diced	
a handful of Chinese cabbage, shredded	
a handful of finely chopped fresh coriander	
2 tbsp vegan mayo	
1 tbsp sesame seeds	
1 tbsp soy sauce	
1 tbsp mirin	
1 tbsp rice wine vinegar	
a pinch each of salt and pepper	

To serve

8 slices vegan smoked cheese
4 vegan brioche rolls
4 tbsp of your favourite burger sauce
4 lettuce leaves
8 rashers vegan 'bacon'

6. To assemble the burger, lightly toast the brioche bun, spread the burger sauce on the bottom bun then add the lettuce leaf. Place two of the smashed patties on top of the lettuce then add two rashers of 'bacon' and some slaw. Finish with a little more burger sauce then place the top bun over the top, securing it in place with a burger skewer to serve.

Pulled 'Pork' Sliders

8 king oyster mushrooms, brushed clean of visible debris

2 tsp smoked paprika

1 tsp black pepper

1 tsp dried sage

1 tsp garlic powder

1 tsp onion powder

½ tsp cayenne pepper

½ tsp salt

2 tbsp The Vurger Co. Smoky 'Bacon' Vegan Mayo or other vegan mayo

To serve

6 mini white rolls or a gluten-free alternative

6 tbsp Smoky 'Bacon' Vegan Mayo or other vegan mayo

mixed salad leaves

mixed slaw

2 spring onions, finely chopped

Mushrooms truly are magical and have so many applications, you won't believe how meaty this king oyster mushroom mix is!

1. Preheat the oven to 200°C fan/400°F/gas 7.

2. Prepare the pulled 'pork' by slicing the tops off each mushroom so you are just left with the stalks (save the tops for another recipe). Hold the stems and use a fork to 'shred' them until they fall apart and resemble a pulled pork texture. Place the shredded mushrooms in a mixing bowl and add the remaining ingredients. Mix well to combine.

3. Place the mushroom mixture on a baking tray lined with parchment paper, spreading it out evenly into a thin layer. Bake the mushrooms in the preheated oven for 25–30 minutes, stirring the mixture halfway through to ensure it all browns evenly.

4. When the mushroom pulled 'pork' is ready, assemble the subs. Slice the white rolls and lightly toast them. Layer on the mayo, spreading it over each roll then add some salad leaves, mixed slaw and the mushroom pulled 'pork'. Finish with a sprinkle of spring onions, the top bun and a skewer to secure everything together.

CHEF'S TIP: baking the pulled mushrooms with mayo acts like an oil but also packs the mushrooms with that little bit more flavour, but you can sub for oil if you'd rather.

SERVES 3 · 30 mins

Cajun 'Shrimp' Popcorn Subs
with Garlic Parsley Sauce

Vegan seafood is something that we have been trying forever to get right, and the pairing of the garlic parsley sauce with the gorgeous crispy Cajun battered hearts of palm really hits the spot for us.

For the garlic parsley sauce

1 tbsp vegan butter
1 tbsp plain flour
120ml (4fl oz) vegan milk
a handful of chopped fresh parsley
a handful of chopped fresh chives
½ tsp salt
½ tsp black pepper
½ tsp garlic powder
1 tbsp nutritional yeast flakes
juice of ½ lemon

For the 'shrimp'

200g (7oz) hearts of palm (drained weight)

For the Cajun batter

½ sheet nori
90g (3¼oz) plain flour
1 tbsp Cajun seasoning
1 tsp salt
175ml (6fl oz) sparkling water, chilled
240ml (8fl oz) oil, for shallow frying

To serve

3 sub rolls
a handful of rocket
sriracha, to taste
3 lemon wedges

1. To make the garlic parsley sauce, gently melt the butter in a small saucepan over a low heat. Add the flour and whisk together to form a thick paste (a roux). Slowly drizzle in the milk, whisking together with the roux until all the milk has been incorporated. You should have a glossy thick sauce. Add the remaining ingredients and whisk together then set aside until ready to serve.

2. For the 'shrimp', cut each of the hearts of palm into 1.5cm (¾ inch) rounds, then push out the centre of each piece until you are left with an 'O' shape. Make a cut from the outer edge of the ring to the centre, so the pieces now form more of a 'C' shape – this will be the base of your 'shrimp'.

3. Make the batter by placing the nori in a blender and blitzing until it turns into a powder. Place in a bowl with 75g (2½oz) of the flour, the Cajun seasoning and the salt and mix together to combine. Pour in the sparkling water and whisk together until it reaches a batter-like consistency.

4. Preheat the oil in a frying pan over a medium heat. To test if the oil is hot enough, place a tiny bit of batter in the oil and if it bubbles and floats to the top, it's ready.

5. Sprinkle the remaining flour evenly over the hearts of palm to fully coat each piece, then place into the hot oil. Shallow fry in batches, for 1 minute each side, until evenly golden brown.

6. When the 'shrimp' are ready, assemble the subs. Slice the sub rolls and layer on the rocket, followed by the Cajun 'shrimp'. Drizzle over the garlic parsley sauce, add a little sriracha, to taste, then squeeze a lemon wedge over the top.

CHEF'S TIP: make sure the batter is kept cold while coating the 'shrimp', otherwise it won't go as light and fluffy.

SERVES 3 · 35 mins · HIGH PROTEIN

Philly Cheesesteak Subs

For the 'steak' mixture

1 tbsp oil

1 white onion, sliced

1 green pepper, sliced into strips

2 vegan burger patties

½ tsp salt

½ tsp black pepper

¾ tsp garlic powder

1 tbsp smoked paprika, plus extra for dusting

2 tbsp ketchup

1 tsp soy sauce

For the mustard cheese sauce

1 tbsp vegan butter

1 tbsp plain flour

150ml (5fl oz) cashew milk

½ tsp salt

½ tsp black pepper

½ tsp smoked paprika

½ tsp onion powder

½ tsp garlic powder

1 tbsp nutritional yeast flakes

1 tsp yellow mustard

40g (1½oz) vegan Cheddar cheese, grated

To serve

3 sub rolls

a handful of salad leaves

This recipe is an adaptation from one of our early special collaborations with Gaz Oakley back in 2019, 'The Philly'. We had to include it in the book as the combination of the meaty sub roll mix and the tangy mustard cheese sauce is just to die for!

1. To make the mustard cheese sauce, gently melt the butter in a small saucepan over a low heat. Add the flour and whisk together to form a thick paste (a roux). Slowly drizzle in the cashew milk, whisking together with the roux until all the milk has been incorporated – this is the base of your cheese sauce. Add the remaining ingredients and whisk together well until the cheese melts and the sauce becomes glossy and thick. Taste and adjust the seasoning if necessary then set aside until ready to serve.

2. To make the 'steak' mixture, preheat the oil in a frying pan over a medium heat then add the onion and fry for about 10 minutes until softened, stirring regularly. Add the green pepper strips and fry for a further 5 minutes until they have a bit of colour.

3. Roughly crumble the burger patties and add to the pan, frying for about 5 minutes until browned. Season well with salt and black pepper then add the garlic powder and smoked paprika, mixing to combine. Add the ketchup and soy sauce and stir together well then fry for a further 2 minutes.

4. To assemble the subs, slice the sub rolls and layer on the salad leaves, then divide the 'steak' mixture evenly between the rolls. Drizzle some mustard cheese sauce over each roll, dust with a little paprika to finish and serve immediately.

CHEF'S TIP: this mustard cheese sauce makes an amazing mac and cheese base. Simply double the recipe and combine with cooked pasta.

SERVES 2-3 | **30 mins** | **GF** | **HIGH PROTEIN**

Nuggets with Crispy 'Chicken Skin'

4 sheets rice paper

2 tbsp 'chicken' salt (see page 118)

200g (7oz) vegan 'chicken' pieces

2 tbsp oil or spray oil

We made a pretty magical discovery when we paired crispy rice paper with vegan 'chicken', and couldn't believe how similar to chicken skin it tasted. We would really recommend using an air fryer to get that super crunchy texture.

1. For best results use an air fryer preheated to 200°C (390°F).

2. If you are not using an air fryer, preheat the oven to 200°C fan/400°F/gas 7.

3. Fill a shallow bowl with water. Cut the rice paper sheets into quarters using scissors then take a quarter sheet and dip it in the bowl of water. Lay the damp rice paper on a clean work surface and sprinkle over a pinch of the 'chicken' salt then place a 'chicken'-style piece on the rice paper.

4. Fold the rice paper around the 'chicken' piece until fully covered then place on a baking tray lined with parchment paper. Repeat until all the pieces of rice paper and 'chicken' are used up.

5. Drizzle or spray the oil over the wrapped 'chicken' pieces and cook for 15 minutes in an air fryer, or 20 minutes in an oven.

6. Serve immediately with our Perfect Fries (see page 116) and your favourite sauce.

CHEF'S TIP: our 'chicken' salt (see page 118) is perfect to season these nuggets, but if you have an alternative spice mix that you love, please feel free to use that instead!

SERVES 4 | 10 mins | GF

Pink Summer Slaw

¼ small red cabbage, finely chopped

¼ small white cabbage, finely chopped

8–10 radishes, shredded

1 carrot, grated

3 tbsp white wine vinegar

3 tbsp vegan mayo

1 tsp caster sugar

½ tsp Dijon mustard

a handful of chopped fresh parsley

a handful of chopped fresh chives

a pinch each of salt and pepper

1. Place all the vegetables in a mixing bowl.

2. Add the vinegar, mayo, sugar and mustard and mix everything together well to fully coat the vegetables.

3. Add the parsley and chives and season well with salt and pepper. Mix again; taste and adjust the seasoning if necessary.

4. Place in an airtight storage container and keep in the fridge until ready to serve.

NUGGETS WITH CRISPY 'CHICKEN SKIN'

PINK SUMMER
SLAW

Butternut Mac 'n' Cheese
with Crispy Sage Breadcrumbs

We feel like a side of mac is essential with any southern-fried 'chicken'-style takeout, and this one ticks all the boxes without feeling too heavy. The butternut squash gives you some goodness while the cashews and the buttery breadcrumb topper add richness – the perfect combination.

For the macaroni cheese

320g (11¼oz) butternut squash, cubed

6 cloves garlic, skin on

oil, for drizzling

1 tsp salt

½ tsp black pepper

350g (12oz) macaroni pasta or a gluten-free alternative

40g (1½oz) raw cashews, soaked

2 tbsp nutritional yeast flakes

1 tsp Dijon mustard

1 tsp paprika

½ tsp onion granules

50g (1¾oz) vegan hard cheese, grated

200ml (7fl oz) vegan milk

juice of ½ lemon

For the breadcrumb topping

2 tbsp vegan butter

8 fresh sage leaves, 4 chopped, 4 whole

35g (1¼oz) breadcrumbs or a gluten-free alternative

1 tbsp oil

CHEF'S TIP : if you've forgotten to soak your cashews for a few hours to get them nice and soft, simply place them in a saucepan of boiling water and simmer for 15 minutes to soften.

1. Preheat the oven to 200°C fan/400°F/gas 7.

2. Place the butternut squash and whole garlic cloves on a baking tray, drizzle with a little oil, and season with the salt and pepper. Place in the preheated oven and bake for about 30 minutes, turning halfway through the cooking time to ensure everything cooks evenly.

3. Meanwhile, cook the macaroni according to the packet instructions in heavily salted water. Drain, reserving a mugful of the pasta water. Set the cooked pasta aside until the butternut squash is cooked.

4. When the butternut squash is cooked and the garlic cloves are soft, remove from the oven. Set aside until the garlic has cooled enough to handle then peel the skin off the garlic. Place the butternut squash, garlic, soaked cashews and all the remaining ingredients, except the pasta and pasta water into a blender and blitz until silky smooth.

5. Place the blended butternut sauce in a saucepan over a low heat and when slightly bubbling, add the cooked pasta. Add about one quarter of the pasta water to the sauce and mix through; add more to thin it out if necessary.

6. Make a quick breadcrumb topping by gently melting the butter in a frying pan. Add the chopped sage and breadcrumbs and cook until lightly toasted. Then set aside until ready to serve.

7. Wipe out the frying pan then add the oil. Place over a medium heat and place the 4 whole sage leaves in the hot oil. Fry until the leaves are crispy, about 2 minutes.

8. To serve, place the butternut macaroni in a pasta bowl and top with the golden breadcrumbs and crispy sage leaves.

SERVES 4–6 as a side · **30 mins** · **GF**

Crispy Corn Ribs
with Chilli Garlic Butter

For the ribs

4 corn on the cob

2 tbsp vegetable oil

1 tsp paprika

½ tsp onion powder

½ tsp garlic powder

For the chilli butter

50g (1¾oz) vegan butter

1 clove garlic, finely chopped

½ tsp chilli flakes

a handful of finely chopped fresh parsley

Another favourite blog recipe which we have levelled up with this gorgeous chilli garlic butter. These are a super addictive side dish, perfect for the warmer months.

1. For best results use an air fryer preheated to 200°C (390°F).

2. If you are not using an air fryer, preheat the oven to 200°C fan/400°F/gas 7.

3. To make the chilli butter, gently melt the butter in a frying pan over a low heat. Add the garlic and chilli flakes and fry in the butter for 2 minutes, until fragrant. Remove from the heat and add the parsley. Pour into a container and place in the fridge until the corn ribs are ready.

4. To make the corn ribs, place a saucepan of water over a medium-high heat to boil. Once boiling, add the corn cobs and par-boil for 5 minutes. Drain and leave to cool slightly until you can handle them.

5. Starting with one piece of corn at a time, hold the corn standing upright, take a sharp knife and cut in half lengthways then in quarters. The core of the cob is super tough so be really careful when cutting. Always keep your fingers away from the blade.

6. Once you have your corn quartered, place it in a bowl and drizzle with the oil then sprinkle over the remaining ingredients.

7. Place the corn cobs in the air fryer or preheated oven and bake for 10–15 minutes.

8. Serve warm, with a teaspoon of the chilli butter on each corn rib.

CHEF'S TIP: using an air fryer will give your ribs that amazing curly appearance but an oven works just as well, you just may need to bake them for 5 minutes longer.

BUTTERNUT
MAC 'N' CHEESE

CRISPY
CORN RIBS

Southern-fried Nuggets

For the crumb

120g (4¼oz) breadcrumbs or gluten-free alternative

95g (3½oz) rice flour

1½ tbsp dried oregano

1 tbsp smoked paprika

1 tbsp chilli flakes

2 tsp black pepper

1½ tsp cayenne pepper

1 tsp salt

1 tsp garlic powder

1 tsp dried mixed herbs

For the batter

2 tbsp chickpea (gram) flour

3 tbsp cornflour

For the 'chicken'

350g (12oz) vegan 'chicken' pieces

3 tbsp oil or spray oil

Inspired by the top-secret crumb which features in all the 'chicken' products on our restaurant menu, we simply had to include a classic crispy nugget within the pages of this book. We love using an air fryer to cook these, but they are incredible deep-fried too.

1. For best results use an air fryer preheated to 200°C (390°F).

2. To make the wet and dry mix for the southern-fried coating, mix all the crumb ingredients together in a mixing bowl. Mix all the batter ingredients together with 100ml (3½fl oz) water in a separate mixing bowl, whisking it until it is smooth and no lumps remain.

3. To crumb the 'chicken' pieces, use one hand for battering, and one hand for the crumb. Take a 'chicken' piece and fully submerge it in the batter then transfer to the crumb and pat the mix onto the 'chicken' piece making sure it is fully coated. Repeat until all the 'chicken' pieces are coated.

4. To cook, add the nuggets to an air fryer, drizzle or spray with the oil and cook for 15 minutes. If deep-frying, heat the oil to 180°C (350°F), and cook for around 4 minutes until golden brown and crispy.

5. Serve hot with your sauce of choice.

Walnut 'Meat' Fries

For the walnut 'meat'

250g (9oz) chestnut mushrooms, cleaned

115g (4oz) walnuts

oil, for frying

50g (1¾oz) roasted red peppers, chopped

3 cloves garlic, minced

1 tbsp paprika

½ tbsp ground cumin

½ tsp chilli powder

1 tbsp tomato purée

1 tbsp agave or maple syrup

juice of ½ lime

To serve

500g (1.1lb) cooked fries

black beans

fresh coriander

tomato salsa

lime wedges

fresh tomatoes

We have always believed in the magic of true wholefood plant-based dishes being able to satisfy you fully, and these walnut 'meat' fries are no exception.

1. Place the mushrooms in a food processor and pulse until they are blitzed to a fine mince. Remove from the processor and repeat the same process with the walnuts.

2. Heat a little oil in a pan over a medium heat, add the minced mushrooms and a pinch each of salt and pepper. Fry for about 10 minutes until the mushrooms are dry and all the water has cooked out.

3. Add the roasted peppers, minced garlic and the spices and fry off for 2 minutes. Add the tomato purée, liquid sweetener and the blitzed walnuts and stir through, then remove from the heat.

4. Assemble everything on a tray: start with the fries then layer over the walnut 'meat'. Add the black beans and the remaining toppings. Serve warm.

SERVES 2 or 4 as a side · 50 mins · HIGH PROTEIN · GF

Truffle Cheese & 'Chorizo' Fries

For the tofu 'chorizo'

200g (7oz) smoked tofu	
3 tsp sweet smoked paprika	
1 tsp cayenne pepper	
½ tsp ground coriander	
½ tsp ground cumin	
1 tsp salt	
1 tsp pepper	
1 tbsp agave or maple syrup	
1 tbsp tomato purée	
1 tsp liquid smoke	
3 tbsp oil	

For the caramelised red onions

2 tbsp oil	
2 red onions, sliced	
1 tsp salt	
1 tbsp balsamic vinegar	
1 tbsp brown sugar	

For the truffle cheese

50g (1¾oz) cashews, soaked	
230ml (7¾fl oz) water	
1 tbsp tapioca starch/flour	
1 tbsp nutritional yeast flakes	
½ tsp onion powder	
1½ tsp refined coconut oil	
1 clove garlic	
1 tsp truffle oil	
1 tsp salt	

To serve

500g (1.1lb) cooked fries	
80g (2¾oz) vegan Cheddar cheese, grated	
fresh chives, chopped	

We have used a beautiful vegan-friendly truffle oil in the house mac 'n' cheese in our restaurants since 2016, and we absolutely love the flavour pairing with the salty and smoky 'chorizo' in this recipe.

1. Preheat the oven to 200°C fan/400°F/gas 7.

2. To make the caramelised onions, heat the oil in a frying pan over a low heat then add the onions and salt. Cook the onions for about 45 minutes, stirring regularly to ensure they are cooking evenly. About half way through the cooking time, add the balsamic vinegar and sugar.

3. Meanwhile, make the tofu 'chorizo' by roughly crumbling the tofu into a mixing bowl.

4. Add the dry ingredients first and mix well, followed by the wet ingredients. Spread the mixture out evenly on a baking tray lined with parchment paper to ensure it gets nice and crispy. Bake in the preheated oven for about 15–20 minutes, or until crispy and slightly charred; keep an eye on it as it will catch easily.

5. While the tofu and onions finish cooking, make the truffle cheese. Add all the ingredients to a high-speed blender and blitz until smooth. Place the mix into a saucepan over a low-medium heat and cook, stirring constantly, for about 3–5 minutes. Once the truffle cheese is thick and has a stretchy consistency it's ready to serve.

6. Now it's time to load everything up! Place the fries on a baking tray and sprinkle over the grated cheese. Place in the hot oven for 5 minutes until the cheese has slightly melted, then start to layer the remaining ingredients. Add the caramelised onions, followed by the truffle cheese and then the tofu 'chorizo'. Return to the oven for a further 2 minutes then remove from the oven, sprinkle over some chopped fresh chives to serve and dig in!

CHEF'S TIP: tapioca starch makes the truffle cheese super stretchy, but if you can't get hold of this then cornflour can work too, you just won't get the same stretchiness!

Gyros-style Fries

For the quick pickled onions

1 red onion, finely sliced

1 tsp salt

1 tbsp sugar

2 tbsp apple cider vinegar

250ml (9fl oz) boiling water

For the 'chicken' shawarma

2 tbsp paprika

1 tsp ground cumin

1 tsp garlic powder

1 tsp ground coriander

1 tsp onion powder

½ tsp ground cinnamon

½ tsp black pepper

½ tsp salt

1 tsp cayenne pepper

2 tbsp oil

190g (6¾oz) vegan 'chicken' pieces

1 tbsp liquid smoke

1 tbsp tomato purée

To serve

500g (1.1lb) cooked fries

60g (2oz) vegan feta

4 tbsp vegan garlic mayo

6 cherry tomatoes, chopped

fresh parsley, chopped

lemon wedges

hot sauce, to taste

The perfect Friday night dinner, these super easy yet indulgent gyros fries will hit every takeout craving. Feel free to add any of your own personal favourite toppings: we absolutely love vegan feta with this.

1. Make the pickled onions first. Place the onions in a heatproof jar and add the salt, sugar and vinegar. Pour in the boiling water until the onions are covered and mix well until everything has dissolved. Place in the fridge while you make the 'chicken' shawarma.

2. To make the shawarma spice mix, place all the spices in a bowl and mix to combine.

3. Heat the oil in a frying pan over a medium heat then add the 'chicken' pieces to the pan and fry for 3–5 minutes until golden. Add 1 tablespoon of the spice mix, the liquid smoke and tomato purée. Mix thoroughly so the 'chicken' pieces are coated evenly, then turn off the heat. If the spice mix starts to stick to the bottom of the frying pan, add a splash of water to loosen everything back up again.

4. Assemble everything on a tray: start with the fries, layer over the shawarma then crumble over the feta. Spoon over the garlic mayo and tomatoes. Take a handful of pickled onions out of the pickle mixture and dry off using kitchen towel. Layer the pickled onions over the top and finish with chopped parsley, lemon wedges and a drizzle of hot sauce to your taste.

CHEF'S TIP: the spice mix for the chicken shawarma is really versatile – so be sure to keep some pre-made in the cupboard, ready to amp up fries or any vegan meat alternative.

TRUFFLE CHEESE & 'CHORIZO' FRIES

GYROS-STYLE
FRIES

SERVES 2 or 4 as a side · 45 mins · GF

Crispy Smashed Potatoes

700g (1.5lb) baby potatoes

2 tbsp oil

1 tbsp dried mixed herbs

1 tbsp garlic powder

a pinch each of salt and pepper

60g (2oz) vegan mayo

To serve

extra vegan mayo

fresh chives and parsley, chopped

Who knew adding vegan mayo to your smashed potatoes made them so crispy and delicious? This is our favourite way to serve baby potatoes.

1. Preheat the oven to 200°C fan/400°F/gas 7.

2. Place the potatoes in a saucepan of water and bring to the boil. Reduce the heat to medium and simmer the potatoes for about 10 minutes, or until they are fork tender. Drain the potatoes and place in a large baking tray. Drizzle with the oil and sprinkle over the mixed herbs, garlic powder, salt and pepper.

3. Using the base of a glass, gently press down on each potato to 'smash' them, so they are about 1cm (½ inch) thick.

4. Place in the preheated oven and bake for 25 minutes, flipping halfway through the cooking time. Remove from the oven and spread the mayo evenly onto each potato then bake for a further 10 minutes until the potatoes are beautifully golden brown.

5. Serve with an extra drizzle of mayo and sprinkle over the chopped fresh herbs.

CHEF'S TIP: these go even crispier in the air fryer!

'Bacon'-loaded Potatoes

3 large potatoes

2 tbsp vegetable oil

2 spring onions, chopped

3 cloves garlic, minced

65g (2¼oz) vegan crème fraîche

40g (1½oz) vegan cheddar, grated

a handful of chopped fresh parsley

1 tbsp nutritional yeast flakes

1 tsp salt

1 tsp pepper

1 tbsp olive oil

To serve

4 rashers cooked vegan 'bacon', chopped

2 tbsp vegan crème fraîche

extra fresh parsley

The perfect lazy dinner, these gorgeous cheesy garlic and bacon-loaded potatoes will fill every comfort food craving you have, and be ready in about 30 minutes.

1. Preheat the oven or an air fryer to 180°C fan/350°F/gas 6.

2. Wash and dry the potatoes, then prick each potato evenly with a fork. Place in the microwave for 15 minutes until soft then set aside until they are cool enough to handle safely. Slice each potato in half lengthways, and scoop out the potato flesh into a bowl, leaving ½cm (¼ inch) of flesh around the potato skins so they keep their shape.

3. Place the remaining ingredients, except the oil, in a mixing bowl along with the scooped out potato flesh and mix everything together well. Spoon the potato mixture back into the potato skins and place on a baking sheet lined with parchment paper. Drizzle over the oil and bake in a preheated oven or air fryer for 10–15 minutes until golden and crispy.

4. Serve with a generous dollop of crème fraîche, crispy 'bacon' and extra fresh chopped parsley.

CHEF'S TIP: Maris Piper potatoes or any other really starchy potatoes work best here.

CRISPY SMASHED
POTATOES

'BACON'-LOADED POTATOES

Perfect Fries

2kg (4.4lbs) Maris Piper potatoes

4 tbsp oil

1 tsp salt, or any of our seasonings (see pages 118–119)

These were born out of a time crunch and not having the time (or inclination!) to par-boil potatoes. This microwave method has changed our lives, and now this is the only chip recipe you'll ever need – perfect fries every time!

1. Preheat the oven or an air fryer to 180°C fan/350°F/gas 6.

2. Wash the potatoes thoroughly to remove any dirt then cut them into 1-cm (½-inch) slices. Lay the slices flat on a chopping board and cut into fries 1cm (½ inch) wide.

3. Place the cut fries in a microwave-safe bowl and cover with clingfilm (you may need to do this in batches). Microwave for 4–6 minutes, depending on the strength of your microwave. This step essentially steams your potatoes, helping them to release moisture before going into the oven or air fryer to crisp up. Be very careful when removing the clingfilm, as the steam that will be released will be very hot. Your fries should be slightly softer but not falling apart.

4. Lay the par-cooked fries on kitchen towels or a clean tea towel to absorb any excess moisture. Pat until the surface of all the fries are dry then place them on a non-stick baking sheet and evenly coat with the oil and salt or other seasoning of your choice.

5. If using an oven, bake for 40 minutes before flipping the fries and cooking for a further 15 minutes.

6. If using an air fryer, cook for 25 minutes, before flipping the fries and cooking for a further 10 minutes, or until golden brown and cooked through.

7. Remove from the oven and serve hot, with your favourite dip.

CHEF'S TIP: you can also deep-fry these if you prefer.

Our Favourite Fries

'Chicken' Salt Fries

A great seasoning to keep in your cupboard and the magic ingredient in our Nuggets with Crispy 'Chicken Skin' recipe (see page 98).

2 tbsp smoked paprika

1 tbsp garlic powder

1 tbsp onion powder

1 tbsp celery salt

1 tsp black pepper

2 tsp dried sage

2 tsp dried parsley

½ tsp dried thyme

1 tsp cayenne pepper

1. Simply combine all the ingredients together in a bowl and mix well.

2. To add to your perfect fries, evenly sprinkle over a tablespoon of seasoning per 1kg (2¼lb) of fries along with your oil, and cook as normal.

3. Store in an airtight storage container for up to 6 months and use to sprinkle over anything!

Garlic Parm Fries

The perfect seasoning for your fries... or anything else!

35g (1¼oz) cashews

20g (¾oz) blanched almonds

60g (2oz) nutritional yeast flakes

1 tsp garlic powder

1 tsp salt

½ tsp onion powder

1. Place all the ingredients in a food processor and blitz to a fine crumb.

2. To add to your perfect fries, evenly sprinkle over 2 tablespoons of seasoning per 1kg (2¼lb) fries when they are 5 minutes away from being perfectly cooked. Make sure the fries are evenly coated then return to the oven for a further 5 minutes. Serve immediately.

3. Store the remaining seasoning in an airtight storage container for up to 1 month.

Spicy Umami Fries

Another staff favourite by our Production Manager Haider, these sticky glazed fries are addictive!

2 tbsp tamari

1 tsp chilli flakes

½ tsp black pepper

½ tsp nigella seeds

1. To make the perfect salty yet spicy fries, follow the steps for Perfect Fries (see page 116).

2. Once the fries have been baking for 20 minutes (or air frying for 10 minutes), remove from the oven and coat evenly with all of the spicy umami ingredients.

3. Return the fries to the oven and cook for the remaining time, until the tamari has turned sticky and coated each of the fries.

4. Serve immediately with your dip of choice.

SPICY UMAMI
FRIES

GARLIC PARM FRIES

'CHICKEN' SALT FRIES

Party Bites

Party Bites

30 Clove Tear & Share Garlic Bread

3 heads garlic

1 tbsp olive oil

1 unsliced loaf of tiger bread

300g (10½oz) vegan butter

a large handful of finely chopped fresh parsley

1 tsp garlic powder

1 tsp salt

1 tsp pepper

100g (3½oz) vegan Cheddar cheese, grated

This is the perfect centrepiece to any party table. In our opinion there is no such thing as too much garlic, but you can always dial back the garlic in this recipe if you're feeling shy.

1. Preheat the oven or to 200°C fan/400°F/gas 7.

2. Slice the tops of each head of garlic to expose all of the bulbs in each head. Drizzle with a little olive oil, then wrap the garlic in foil. Bake in the preheated oven for 45 minutes.

3. Meanwhile, make diagonal slices vertically along the bread, going nearly to the base but not cutting all the way through. Make the slices about 2.5cm (1 inch) thick, going in one direction. Then make diagonal slices going horizontally in the other direction, again not cutting all the way through – this will create your tear and share pieces.

4. Gently melt the butter in a saucepan over a low heat or in a microwave, then place in a bowl with the parsley, garlic powder, salt and pepper. Mix to combine.

5. Remove the garlic from the oven and set aside until it is cool enough to handle, then squeeze the soft roasted garlic out of each of the heads and roughly chop it into a purée. Add to the melted butter and mix well.

6. Pour the butter over the sliced bread, making sure it gets in all of the gaps and soaks into all the exposed bread. Repeat this until you have about 20% of the butter mixture left. Fill in the gaps of the bread evenly with the grated cheese. Pour the remaining butter mixture over the top of the bread and cover with foil.

7. Place in the hot oven for 10 minutes, then remove the foil and bake for another 5 minutes, until the cheese is melted and the bread slightly golden. Serve immediately.

CHEF'S TIP: you can always make the garlic butter ahead of time and keep it in the fridge to accompany any other dish of your choice.

SERVES 8-10 | 60 mins

Giant Miso Sausage Roll

For the filling

1 tbsp vegan butter

1 red onion, finely chopped

1 leek, finely chopped

1 cooking apple, peeled and grated

4 cloves garlic, minced

1 tsp dried sage

1 tsp black pepper

a pinch of salt

1 tbsp smoked paprika

½ tsp chilli flakes

2 tbsp balsamic vinegar

2 tbsp miso paste

8 vegan sausages

100g (3½oz) breadcrumbs

For the pastry

1 sheet puff pastry

1 tbsp maple syrup

1 tbsp oil

Miso and apple pair perfectly with sage and sausage flavours, and this is what makes this giant sausage roll a real crowd-pleaser. Feel free to make this mix into mini sausage rolls or whatever shape you fancy!

1. Preheat the oven to 200°C fan/400°F/gas 7.

2. Melt the butter in a frying pan over a medium heat then add the onion and leek and fry for about 7 minutes until softened, stirring often. Add the grated apple, garlic and all the seasonings and fry for another 2 minutes. Then add the balsamic vinegar and miso paste and turn off the heat.

3. Remove the 'skin' from the sausages and crumble them into a mixing bowl. Add the fried vegetables and mix together well. Finally, add the breadcrumbs to firm up the mixture and mix again to combine. Cover and place in the fridge while you prepare the pastry.

4. Unroll the sheet of puff pastry onto a baking sheet lined with parchment paper. Place the sausage filling lengthways on one half of the pastry sheet, spreading it out evenly and pressing it down with your hands to make sure it's nice and compact. Then fold the other half of the pastry over the top of the filling. Seal along the edge by pressing the tines of a fork into the pastry or crimp together with your fingers. Score the pastry a couple of times on the top; this will allow some steam to escape and for the sausage roll to cook evenly.

5. Mix the maple syrup and oil together in a small bowl and brush it over the top of the sausage roll using a pastry brush. Place in the preheated oven and bake for 30–35 minutes, or until golden brown.

6. Leave to cool for 10 minutes, then cut into slices and serve. It's delicious hot or cold.

CHEF'S TIP: we would recommend using really 'meaty' vegan sausages for this, not vegetable-based ones. They hold their shape and make for a much better bite in the sausage roll.

'Lobster' Bruschetta

100g (3½oz) pink oyster mushrooms, brushed clean of visible debris

2 tbsp apple cider vinegar

1 tsp salt

110g (4oz) hearts of palm, finely diced

100g (3½oz) jarred red pepper, finely diced

1 stick celery, finely diced

1 sheet nori, blended to a powder

1 tsp vegan fish sauce

juice of 1 lemon

½ tsp black pepper

½ tsp salt

To serve

1 baguette, sliced

lemon wedges

fresh dill

When we made this recipe for our blog, it was our most clicked on recipe throughout all of the Christmas period. Since then we have levelled up the recipe and know this will be a staple in your party food repertoire. If you can't find pink oyster mushrooms simply swap them out for regular oyster mushrooms, the pink is purely for colour.

1. Put the mushrooms in a saucepan with 400ml (14fl oz) water, the apple cider vinegar and salt (and beetroot juice, if using, see Chef's Tip below). Bring to the boil and simmer for 5–6 minutes.

2. Meanwhile, place the hearts of palm, red peppers and celery in a mixing bowl.

3. Drain the mushrooms and squeeze any excess water from them. Tear the mushrooms up into chunky pieces and add them to the bowl along with the remaining ingredients. Mix well and place in the fridge for 30 minutes to chill.

4. Preheat the grill.

5. To serve, place the baguette slices on a baking tray and place under the grill to lightly toast.

6. Spread the 'lobster' mix onto the toasted bread slices and serve with fresh dill and lemon wedges.

CHEF'S TIP: if you use regular oyster mushrooms but still want that pink colour, you can add a little beetroot juice to the mix when boiling.

Macancini Balls

145g (5oz) macaroni or small shape pasta, or a gluten-free alternative

120g (4½oz) vegan mozzarella, cubed

For the mushroom mix

2 tbsp oil

200g (7oz) button mushrooms, cleaned and finely minced

¼ leek, finely diced

½ small white onion, finely diced

4 cloves garlic, minced

1 tsp salt

½ tsp black pepper

For the white sauce

50g (1¾oz) vegan butter

50g (1¾oz) plain white flour

80ml (2¾fl oz) vegan cream

2 tbsp nutritional yeast flakes

400ml (14fl oz) vegan milk

juice of ½ lemon

salt and pepper, to taste

We have been making vegan mac 'n' cheese since 2016, so we'd like to think we've cracked the code by now! This perfect fusion of macaroni cheese with risotto flavours is a dream come true.

1. To make the mushroom mix, heat the oil in a frying pan over a medium heat, add the mushrooms, leek, onion and garlic and fry for 5 minutes. Stir in the salt and pepper and cook for a further 5 minutes, then set aside to cool.

2. Cook the pasta according to the packet instructions. Drain and cool with cold water and set aside until needed.

3. To make the white sauce, gently melt the butter in a saucepan over a low heat. Gradually add the flour and whisk together to form a thick paste (a roux). Slowly add the cream, whisking it together with the roux until it is fully incorporated. Add the nutritional yeast flakes then slowly pour in the milk, whisking continuously so the mixture has no lumps.

4. Add the white sauce to the mushroom mix and stir through. Then add the cooked pasta and stir through. Place in the fridge to chill for 30 minutes.

5. When the mix has chilled, take a small handful in the palm of your hand and push a cube of vegan mozzarella into the centre. Roll the mixture around the mozzarella until it forms a ball. Continue until all the mix has been rolled into balls, place the balls into a freezer-proof container and freeze for about 1 hour until the mixture has firmed up.

6. Preheat an air fryer or a deep fat fryer to 180°C (350°F).

7. To make the crumb coating, combine the rice flour, breadcrumbs, dried mixed herbs, salt, black pepper and nutritional yeast flakes in a bowl.

For the crumb coating

60g (2oz) rice flour

60g (2oz) breadcrumbs or gluten-free alternative

1½ tsp dried mixed herbs

½ tsp salt

1½ tsp black pepper

3 tsp nutritional yeast flakes

For the batter

3 tbsp chickpea (gram) flour

4 tbsp cornflour

To serve

2 tbsp grated vegan Parmesan

fresh parsley, chopped

your favourite tomato sauce, for dipping

8. To make the batter, place the gram flour and cornflour in a bowl with 90ml (3fl oz) water. Whisk the mixture thoroughly to make sure there are no lumps.

9. Remove the macancini balls from the freezer and dip each in turn into the batter then into the crumb coating, making sure the balls are fully covered. Repeat so each ball is double coated. Alternatively, deep fry them for 5 minutes. Alternatively, this is a great recipe to make in advance, simply pop them back in the freezer until your party so they are ready to cook straight away.

10. When all the balls have been crumbed, spray with a little cooking oil and place in an air fryer for 20 minutes, or until golden, turning them over halfway through.

11. Before serving, sprinkle the macancini balls with grated Parmesan, some fresh parsley and serve with your favourite tomato sauce.

CHEF'S TIP: to get the perfect shape with each ball, use an ice cream scoop to evenly form each one.

MAKES 8 · 45 mins

Pesto & Ricotta Twists

For the vegan 'ricotta'

250g (9oz) firm tofu, drained and patted dry

2 tbsp nutritional yeast flakes

2 tbsp hummus

juice of ½ lemon

½ tsp Dijon mustard

¼ tsp black pepper

¼ tsp onion powder

a pinch of salt

To assemble

1 sheet puff pastry

80g (2¾oz) vegan pesto

60g (2oz) vegan mozzarella cheese, grated

To glaze

1 tbsp vegetable oil

1 tbsp maple syrup

These are a real crowd-pleaser, and the vegan ricotta alone has so many applications. Most shop-bought puff pastry is accidentally vegan but just check the ingredients!

1. Preheat the oven to 180°C fan/350°F/gas 6.

2. To make the ricotta, drain and pat dry the block of tofu using kitchen towels or a clean tea towel. Place the tofu in a food processor and blitz until it reaches a smooth consistency.

3. Add the remaining ricotta ingredients and blitz once more to combine everything together.

4. Unroll the sheet of puff pastry onto a baking sheet lined with parchment paper. Spoon the ricotta mix evenly over half of the puff pastry, lengthways. Layer the pesto over the top of the ricotta, sprinkle the vegan cheese over the top of the pesto then fold the other half of the pastry over the top of the filling.

5. Cut the folded pastry into 2.5-cm (1-inch) wide slices. Hold the sliced pieces at each end and twist so the pastry forms a twist in the middle. Twist it round twice to get a nice spiral shape.

6. Space each twist out on the baking sheet so they have enough space to rise. Make the glaze in a small bowl by mixing together the oil and maple syrup and brush over each pastry twist.

7. Place in the preheated oven for 20–25 minutes until golden brown and risen. Serve hot or cold.

CHEF'S TIP: the mixture of maple syrup and oil makes a great replacement for an egg wash over the pastry, golden and flaky pastry every time.

'Calamari' Rings
with Tartar Sauce

For the 'calamari'

6 king oyster mushrooms, brushed clean of any debris

1 tbsp vegan fish sauce

juice of ½ lemon

2 tbsp caper brine

For the crumb coating

3 tbsp plain flour

3 tbsp breadcrumbs

½ tsp celery salt

For the tartar sauce

100g (3½oz) vegan mayo

1 tsp agave syrup

1 tsp capers, diced

juice of ¼ lemon

a pinch of dried dill

a pinch of black pepper

250ml (9fl oz) oil, for shallow frying (alternatively you can use an air fryer)

Mushrooms are an amazing replacement for so many things, but the stems of oyster mushrooms have that almost bouncy texture that really gives a calamari feel.

1. Slice the mushroom stems into 1-cm (½-inch) thick slices. Reserve the heads of the mushrooms for another recipe. Make a hole in the centre of each mushroom slice, (see Chef's Tip, below) leaving about ½-cm (¼-inch) width 'O' shape – this is the base of your 'calamari'.

2. Place your mushroom pieces in a bowl and add the fish sauce, lemon juice and caper brine. Mix together and leave to marinate for 10–15 minutes but no longer, otherwise the mushrooms will become mushy.

3. While the mushrooms are marinating, mix all the tartar sauce ingredients together in a bowl until fully incorporated. Place in the fridge until ready to serve.

4. To make the crumb coating, place the flour, breadcrumbs and celery salt in a mixing bowl and stir to combine.

5. When the mushrooms have marinated, place them into the breadcrumb mixture and pat the mix onto the 'calamari' pieces to coat them.

6. To shallow fry, preheat the oil in a deep frying pan to 180°C (350°F) and carefully drop the 'calamari' into the hot oil. Fry for about 2 minutes, turning halfway through the cooking time to make sure they are all equally golden.

7. To air fry, preheat an air fryer to 180°C (350°F). Place the 'calamari' into the air fryer and spray with a little oil. Cook for 5–7 minutes until crispy.

8. Serve immediately with the tartar sauce and enjoy.

CHEF'S TIP: a circular piping bag nozzle works really well to make the holes in each calamari piece.

'Crackling' Bites
with Sticky Umami Glaze

4 sheets rice paper

250ml (9fl oz) oil, for shallow frying (alternatively you can use an air fryer)

For the 'crackling' seasoning

1 tbsp smoked paprika

½ tsp garlic powder

1 tsp onion powder

1 tsp dried sage

1 tsp salt

1 tsp caster sugar

¼ tsp chilli powder

For the sticky umami glaze

2 tbsp soy sauce or tamari

2 tbsp agave syrup

1 tbsp liquid smoke

1 tbsp balsamic vinegar

1 tbsp miso paste

½ tsp garlic powder

1 tbsp paprika

Our most popular restaurant special to date was our 'Pork Crackling' burger, and now we are spilling the secrets on how we made that incredible 'crackling' that everyone loved!

1. Mix all the 'crackling' seasoning ingredients together in a bowl to combine.

2. Place all the ingredients for the sticky glaze in a separate mixing bowl and whisk until incorporated.

3. To assemble the 'crackling', fill a shallow bowl with water and place it next to the bowl containing the seasoning mix. Dip a sheet of rice paper into the water then place it on a clean work surface. Sprinkle over a teaspoon of the 'crackling' seasoning mix to evenly cover the rice paper.

4. Repeat this process by dipping another rice paper sheet in the water and lay this on top of the first seasoned sheet. Sprinkle with another teaspoon of the seasoning mix and repeat this process with the last two sheets of rice paper, stacking each one on top of the previous sheets.

5. Cut the rice paper stack into around 15 different-shaped small triangles, they don't have to be neat.

6. To shallow fry, preheat the oil in a deep frying pan to 180°C (350°F) and carefully drop the 'crackling' into the hot oil. Fry for about 2 minutes, turning halfway through the cooking time to make sure they are all equally golden.

7. To air fry, preheat an air fryer to 180°C (350°F). Place the 'crackling' into the air fryer and spray with a little oil. Cook for 5–7 minutes until crispy.

8. To serve, dip the 'crackling' into the glaze and serve immediately.

CHEF'S TIP: once cooked, these freeze really well. Simply pop back in the oven or air fryer for 5 minutes before serving.

'CALAMARI' RINGS

'CRACKLING' BITES

MAKES 14 · **20 mins** · **GFO**

Haider's Party Pakoras

1 potato, peeled and finely sliced

1 white onion, finely sliced

a handful of spinach, roughly chopped

1 litre (34fl oz) vegetable oil, for frying

For the pakora batter

1 tbsp coriander seeds

1 tsp cumin seeds

100g (3½oz) chickpea (gram) flour

50g (1¾oz) plain flour, or gluten-free plain flour

1 tsp salt

1 tsp ground coriander

½ tsp chilli flakes

¼ tsp chilli powder

¼ tsp ground turmeric

½ tsp baking powder

For the mint yoghurt

150g (5¼oz) vegan yoghurt

1 tbsp mint sauce

½ tsp onion powder

½ tsp garlic powder

½ tsp agave syrup

a pinch each of salt and pepper

This recipe is by our very own Production Manager, Haider, who makes us the most incredible food not only for our restaurants but for us at lunchtimes too! We always knew it was a special occasion when the pakoras came out – they were devoured in 5 minutes!

1. Cut the potato slices into matchstick-sized fries and set aside.

2. To make the pakora batter, place the coriander and cumin seeds in a mortar and roughly crush using a pestle then place in a mixing bowl. Add the remaining dry batter ingredients and mix to combine. Add 70ml (2½fl oz) water and whisk together until you have a thick sticky batter and no lumps remain. Add the potato matchsticks, onion and spinach and mix well.

3. To make the yoghurt, simply combine all the ingredients together in a small bowl and place in the fridge until ready to serve.

4. Preheat the oil in a deep frying pan to 180°C (350°F) then carefully drop a heaped tablespoon of the pakora mixture into the oil. Fry in batches of about 6–7 pakoras at a time – try not to overcrowd the pan. Fry for 2 minutes on each side until golden.

5. Drain and place on a plate lined with kitchen towel to absorb any excess oil. Sprinkle with a little salt and serve immediately with the mint yoghurt.

CHEF'S TIP: you can use any vegetables you like in the pakora mix, these are just our favourites!

MAKES 20 · **60 mins** · **GFO**

Jackfruit Jalapeño Poppers

A RECIPE BY CHEF GAZ OAKLEY

10 large jalapeño peppers or sweet peppers, cut in half lengthways, seeds removed

For the jackfruit filling

2 x 400g (14oz) tins young jackfruit in brine, drained

1 tbsp garlic powder

1 tbsp smoked paprika

3 spring onions, finely chopped

a handful of finely chopped fresh coriander

1 tbsp hot sauce of your choice

1 tbsp miso paste

1 tsp sea salt

For the rest of the toppings

120g (4¼oz) vegan Cheddar cheese, grated

85g (3oz) panko breadcrumbs or a gluten-free alternative

2 tbsp olive oil

To serve

lime wedges

fresh coriander, finely chopped

These poppers are a huge crowd-pleaser, simply swap out jalapeños for sweet peppers if you're spice averse! Perfect served with any of our sauces.

1. Preheat the oven to 180°C fan/350°F/gas 6.

2. To make the filling, place the jackfruit into a nut-milk bag or clean tea towel and twist and squeeze to expel as much water as you can. This will create extra 'meaty' jackfruit pieces. Once the jackfruit is dry, shred it and place it in a mixing bowl with the remainder of the filling ingredients and mix well.

3. Place the halved jalapeños on a baking tray, cut side up. Spoon as much of the jackfruit filling into each jalapeño as you can then top each one with a sprinkle of the grated cheese. Top each jalapeño with some breadcrumbs and drizzle over a little olive oil.

4. Place the stuffed peppers in the preheated oven on the middle shelf and bake for 25–30 minutes. Serve immediately with lime wedges and a sprinkle of freshly chopped coriander.

CHEF'S TIP: remove any hard parts of the jackfruit that don't shred as easily.

MAKES 20

30 mins

+1½ hours

Smoked 'Salmon' Canapés

For the smoked 'salmon'

4 large carrots, scrubbed clean

1 tbsp salt

For the marinade

½ sheet nori

1 tsp vegan fish sauce

1 tsp soy sauce

2 tsp agave syrup

¼ tsp black pepper

¼ tsp paprika

juice of ½ lemon

To serve

150g (5¼oz) vegan cream cheese

20 small crackers

fresh dill, finely chopped

lemon wedges

When carrots are slow-roasted and marinated, they make the most magical fish replacement. This simple swap served on cream cheese crackers really hits the spot.

1. Preheat the oven to 200°C fan/400°F/gas 7.

2. There is no need to peel the carrots beforehand, simply place them on a baking tray and sprinkle the salt over them. Place in the preheated oven and bake for 35 minutes, or until the carrots are tender. Remove from the oven and set aside to cool while you make the marinade.

3. Blitz the sheet of nori in a food processor until it turns to a fine powder. Place the nori powder in a mixing bowl with the remaining marinade ingredients and 100ml (3½fl oz) water.

4. When the carrots are cool, use a Y-peeler to create ribbons from the carrots. Place the carrot ribbons in the marinade and place in the fridge to chill for at least 1 hour 30 minutes (see Chef's Tip).

5. To assemble the smoked 'salmon' canapés, spread the cream cheese onto the crackers and place on a serving plate. Layer over the smoked 'salmon' carrots then sprinkle over some fresh chopped dill. Finish by placing lemon wedges on the plate for guests to squeeze over.

CHEF'S TIP: these are best made the day before so the marinade fully infuses into the carrots.

MAKES 20–30 | 30 mins +1 hour | GFO

Cajun Shroom Dippers

150g (5¼oz) oyster mushrooms, brushed clean of any debris

3 tbsp rice flour

250ml (9fl oz) vegetable oil, for shallow frying

For the crumb

150g (5¼oz) breadcrumbs or a gluten-free alternative

1 tbsp garlic powder

1 tbsp chilli powder

1 tbsp paprika

2 tsp onion powder

2 tsp black pepper

1½ tsp chilli flakes

1 tsp salt

½ tsp dried thyme

For the batter

2 tbsp chickpea (gram) flour

3 tbsp cornflour

Shroom dippers were an absolute staple side dish in our restaurants for years and we are constantly asked to add them back onto the menu. Until we can do just that – here's how to recreate them at home.

1. Cut any larger mushrooms in half so they are all of a similar size. Place into a bowl and coat with the rice flour.

2. To make the wet and dry mix for the coating, mix all the crumb ingredients together in a mixing bowl. Mix all the batter ingredients together with 100ml (3½fl oz) water in a separate mixing bowl, whisking it until it is smooth and no lumps remain.

3. To crumb the mushrooms, use one hand for battering, and one hand for the crumb. Take a piece of mushroom and fully submerge it in the batter to coat it evenly, then transfer to the crumb and pat the mix onto the mushroom, making sure it is fully coated. Repeat until all the mushroom pieces are coated.

4. Place the coated mushrooms in the freezer for 1 hour, or until you are ready to cook and serve.

5. Heat the oil in a shallow frying pan over a medium heat. Add the breaded mushrooms and fry for 3–4 minutes until golden brown all over. Remove from the oil and place on a plate lined with kitchen towel to absorb any excess oil.

6. Sprinkle with salt and serve immediately with your favourite sauce.

CHEF'S TIP: these are perfect served with our Buffalo Aioli on page 185 for that spicy kick!

Desserts & Drinks

Desserts & Drinks

MAKES 12 | 30 mins +1 hour | GF

Notella Truffles

400g (14oz) tin coconut milk, refrigerated

180g (6¼oz) vegan dark chocolate

45g (1½oz) golden syrup

a pinch of salt

100g (3½oz) ground hazelnuts

20g (¾oz) roasted whole hazelnuts

These are reminiscent of a very famous chocolate hazelnut truffle... and inspired by our chocolate hazelnut milkshake. Careful though, they're addictive!

1. Ensure your coconut milk has fully set in the fridge before use, so that the thick coconut cream separates from the coconut water.

2. Melt the dark chocolate together with the golden syrup and a pinch of salt in a bowl set over a pan of simmering water or in a bain-marie.

3. Carefully open the tin of coconut milk and weigh out 90g (3¼oz) of the solidified coconut cream (reserve the coconut water for another recipe). Add the coconut cream to the bowl of melted chocolate and continue to heat, stirring gently, until this melts also.

4. Place the coconut chocolate mixture in the fridge to cool and firm up, this should take about 1 hour.

5. Meanwhile, place the ground hazelnuts in a bowl.

6. Once the truffle mixture is firm enough to handle, scoop a tablespoon of the mixture into your palm, then press a whole hazelnut into the centre.

7. Mould the chocolate truffle mixture around the whole hazelnut and roll between your palms to form the truffle so the hazelnut is fully encased.

8. Roll each truffle in the ground hazelnuts until fully coated.

9. Repeat this process with the remaining mixture until it has all been used up.

CHEF'S TIP: these will keep in an airtight storage container in the fridge for 1 week... if they last that long!

Banoffee Millionaire's Shortbread

For the shortbread

180g (6¼oz) plain flour

40g (1½oz) plus 2 tbsp caster sugar

90g (3¼oz) vegan butter, cut into small cubes and chilled

2 tbsp vegan milk

For the caramel bananas

150g (5¼oz) light brown sugar

150g (5¼oz) caster sugar

200g (7oz) vegan butter

½ tsp salt

2 tbsp golden syrup

250ml (9fl oz) vegan cream

2 bananas, peeled and sliced widthways

For the topping

200g (7oz) vegan dark chocolate

20g (¾oz) dried banana chips

You will see a lot of inspiration from our restaurant milkshake flavours in this section, and this twist on one of our favourite childhood desserts is no exception. Our caramel is also adapted from when we first opened our market stall back in 2016 and used to serve hot chocolate brownies with the caramel – absolute heaven.

1. To make the shortbread, sift the flour into a mixing bowl and add the 40g (1½oz) sugar and chilled cubes of butter. Using your fingertips, rub the butter into the flour and sugar until the mix turns into a fine crumb. Add the milk 1 tablespoon at a time and rub the mixture together again. This should be just enough milk to bring the mixture together into a ball. If the mixture comes together after just 1 tablespoon of milk, don't add the second tablespoon. On the other hand, if your mixture is still crumbly after 2 tablespoons, add a splash more milk until the mixture comes together.

2. Place the shortbread mixture in a 20x20-cm (8x8-inch) baking dish lined with parchment paper and press the mixture evenly into the dish using your fingers, making sure to press evenly into every edge of the dish. Cover the shortbread with clingfilm and place in the fridge to chill for about 30 minutes before baking.

3. Meanwhile, make the caramel bananas. Place both the sugars, the butter, salt and golden syrup in a saucepan over a medium heat. Stir the mixture until everything has melted together, then add the cream.

4. Place a sugar thermometer into the pan and keep stirring the mixture until the temperature reaches 110°C (230°F). Remove the pan from the heat and set aside.

5. Preheat the oven to 180°C fan/350°F/gas 6.

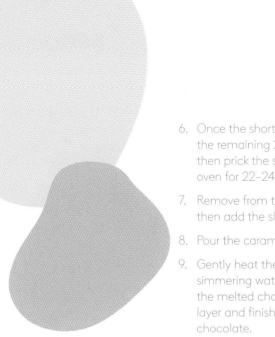

6. Once the shortbread has rested, remove the clingfilm and sprinkle the remaining 2 tablespoons of caster sugar over the shortbread then prick the surface all over with a fork. Bake in the preheated oven for 22–24 minutes.

7. Remove from the oven and set aside to cool for about 10 minutes, then add the sliced bananas in a layer over the top.

8. Pour the caramel over the sliced bananas.

9. Gently heat the dark chocolate in a bowl set over a pan of simmering water or in a bain-marie until melted and glossy. Pour the melted chocolate evenly over the top of the caramel banana layer and finish by placing the banana chips on top of the melted chocolate.

10. Place in the fridge for at least 30 minutes until all the layers have set and it is ready to slice. Use a very sharp knife to cut it evenly into 9 squares.

11. These will keep in an airtight storage container in the fridge for 7 days.

CHEF'S TIP: the caramel will harden as it cools so don't worry if it's on the thinner side when you pour it on top of the shortbread, once it sets in the fridge it will firm up.

Chocolate Orange Tiffin
with Candied Orange Slices

For the tiffin

1 large orange

80g (2¾oz) vegan butter

200g (7oz) vegan dark chocolate, broken into small pieces

80g (2¾oz) golden syrup

240g (8½oz) digestive biscuits or a gluten-free alternative

70g (2½oz) mixed nuts, roughly chopped

a pinch of salt

For the candied orange slices

1 large orange

3 tbsp caster sugar

Every Christmas in the restaurant we launch three new shake flavours, and the one we bring back time and time again is our chocolate orange shake. Customers loved it so much we even launched a low waste advent calendar in this flavour. Perfect over the festive period, this tiffin also makes a gorgeous gift for loved ones.

1. Start by making the candied orange slices. Cut the orange into slices ½ cm (¼ inch) thick. Heat the caster sugar and 3 tablespoons of water in a frying pan over a low heat until the sugar has melted to form a simple syrup. Lay the orange slices in the syrup and keep over a low heat for about 30 minutes, turning them over halfway through the cooking time. You will know they are candied when they turn a golden orange colour and are super glossy.

2. To make the tiffin, zest the orange and place the orange zest in a heatproof mixing bowl. Set the bowl over a pan of simmering water and add the butter and dark chocolate. Mix until melted and fully incorporated then remove from the heat. Add the golden syrup and mix together. Cut the zested orange in half and squeeze the juice into the bowl, stirring it into the mix.

3. Crush the digestive biscuits into a crumb, leaving some larger pieces to give the tiffin some crunch. Add the digestives and mixed nuts to the chocolate mix, along with a pinch of salt and stir to combine.

4. Spoon the tiffin mixture into a 20x20-cm (8x8-inch) baking dish lined with parchment paper and spread it out evenly, pressing the mix into each corner of the dish. Lay the candied orange pieces evenly over the top of the tiffin mixture then place in the fridge to firm up for 30 minutes.

5. Use a sharp knife to cut into 9 even slices. These will keep in an airtight storage container in the fridge for 7 days.

MAKES 15 · 30 mins · GF

Honeycomb Shards

170g (6oz) caster sugar

85g (3oz) golden syrup

1 tsp bicarbonate of soda

100g (3½oz) vegan dark chocolate

Another simple dessert that makes a really good gift. We discovered vegan honeycomb when we launched our vegan 'honey'-themed menu items in honour of our Manchester store opening and have been obsessed ever since.

1. Place the sugar, golden syrup and 60ml (2fl oz) water in a saucepan over a medium heat. Stir everything together then place a sugar thermometer into the mix and do not stir again.

2. Heat the mix until it reaches 120°C (250°F) on the thermometer, which is when it will form a caramel. Keep a close eye on the mix and as soon as it has reached the correct temperature add the bicarb and whisk it into the mix thoroughly. The mixture will start to go really bubbly.

3. As soon as this happens, transfer the mixture to a baking sheet lined with parchment paper to set.

4. Gently melt the dark chocolate in a heatproof bowl in the microwave at 20-second intervals, stirring in between to make sure the chocolate doesn't burn, then pour the melted chocolate over the top of the honeycomb. Place in the fridge to set for 15 minutes.

5. When set, break the honeycomb up into into approximately 15 shards either using a knife or with your hands.

CHEF'S TIP: be careful when adding your bicarb to the sugar mixture as it will bubble a lot, and make sure you stir this really quickly and get it straight into the tray, it sets fast!

Fudgy Oreo Muffins

120ml (4fl oz) oil
400ml (14fl oz) tinned coconut milk
250g (9oz) brown sugar
2 tbsp vanilla extract
200g (7oz) vegan dark chocolate
350g (12oz) self-raising flour
1 tsp baking powder
100g (3½oz) Oreos, crushed, plus 16 whole Oreos
½ tsp salt

Our bestselling shake has always been the Oreo, so we couldn't not pay homage to it in muffin form. These couldn't be simpler to make.

1. Preheat the oven to 180°C fan/350°F/gas 6.

2. Place the oil, coconut milk, brown sugar and vanilla extract in a mixing bowl and whisk together.

3. Gently melt the dark chocolate in a heatproof bowl in the microwave at 20-second intervals, stirring in between to make sure the chocolate doesn't burn, then add the melted chocolate to the mixing bowl and whisk together.

4. Sift in the flour, baking powder, crushed Oreos and salt and mix together.

5. Line a muffin tray with 16 muffin cases, and evenly distribute the mixture between the cases.

6. Push one whole Oreo into each muffin case, pushing down so that the muffin mixture comes up over the top of each Oreo.

7. Bake in the preheated oven for 15 minutes until the muffins are risen and fluffy.

8. Remove from the oven and leave to cool for 5 minutes. Serve warm or cold.

CHEF'S TIP: this also makes for a great traybake chocolate cake if you don't want to make muffins! Just bake for an extra 5 minutes.

PB & J
Mayo Mug Cake

5 tbsp self-raising flour

½ tsp baking powder

1 tbsp brown sugar

1 tbsp caster sugar

1 tsp vanilla extract

1 tbsp vegan butter

1 tbsp vegan mayo

1 tbsp peanut butter

2 tbsp vegan milk

1 tbsp raspberry jam

Our restaurants are proudly peanut free to ensure our menu is super allergen friendly, but that doesn't mean that we aren't inundated with requests to make a peanut butter shake! This super simple mug cake can also be made with almond butter too, and is ideal if you want a lazy dessert after a long day.

1. Place all the dry ingredients in a microwave-safe mug.

2. Add the remaining wet ingredients, except the raspberry jam, and cream them together until everything is incorporated.

3. Make a small well in the middle of the mix and spoon the raspberry jam into the well. Cover over the jam with the mixture and place the mug in the microwave.

4. Microwave on full power for 80–90 seconds until the mixture has doubled in size and is fluffy.

5. Leave to stand for a further 30 seconds, then dig in!

CHEF'S TIP: we know adding mayo sounds unlikely, but this creates the most incredible light and airy texture, it's the perfect egg replacer!

Biscoff Cookies

75g (2½oz) vegan butter

90g (3¼oz) Biscoff spread

75g (2½oz) brown sugar

1 tsp vanilla extract

175g (6oz) plain flour

½ tsp baking powder

½ tsp salt

1 tbsp vegan milk

65g (2¼oz) vegan chocolate chips

To serve

1 tbsp Biscoff spread, melted

a pinch of sea salt flakes

One of our bestselling shakes is the iconic Biscoff, and we totally know why! These cookies are inspired by that shake flavour and are a super low-effort dessert.

1. Cream together the margarine, Biscoff spread, brown sugar and vanilla extract using a hand-held electric whisk until soft. Sift in the flour, baking powder and salt and mix everything together well. Drizzle in the milk to loosen the mixture slightly. You may need a little more milk depending on the temperature of the margarine. Finally, fold in the chocolate chips.

2. Form the mixture into golf ball-sized balls, about 75g (2½oz) each, and place on a baking sheet lined with parchment paper. Place in the fridge to chill for 30 minutes.

3. Preheat the oven to 180°C fan/350°F/gas 6.

4. When chilled, flatten out the dough balls with the palm of your hand to form a disc; these don't have to be perfect as they will expand further in the oven.

5. Bake in the preheated oven for 12–14 minutes, or until lightly browned. The cookies will feel really soft when they come out of the oven but will firm up as they cool.

6. Drizzle the melted Biscoff spread over the cookies then sprinkle over a few sea salt flakes before serving.

CHEF'S TIP: the great thing about vegan cookies is that you can eat the cookie dough raw! Just make sure you buy heat-treated flour instead.

Frozen Strawberry Cheesecake Bars

For the biscuit base

150g (5¼oz) digestive biscuits or gluten-free alternative

50g (1¾oz) vegan butter

For the cheesecake layer

375g (13oz) vegan cream cheese

4 tbsp cornflour

1 tbsp vanilla extract

a pinch of salt

150g (5¼oz) icing sugar

For the strawberry layer

150g (5¼oz) frozen strawberries

25g (1oz) caster sugar

80g (2¾oz) fresh strawberries, sliced, 3 reserved for decoration

CHEF'S TIP: this recipe also works perfectly in cupcake moulds as little individual cheesecake bites, just be sure to line the moulds with cases so they can be removed easily.

We often find that vegan cheesecakes are super complicated with tonnes of ingredients we don't have in stock, so we wanted to make something simple that you could easily whip up at home and enjoy on a hot day.

1. To make the biscuit base, crush the digestive biscuits to a fine crumb by placing them in a sandwich bag and rolling over the bag with a rolling pin or glass bottle.

2. Gently melt the butter in a bowl in the microwave for 20 seconds or in a saucepan over a low heat, then add to the crushed digestives. Mix together until evenly incorporated.

3. Line a loaf tin with parchment paper then add the biscuit base to the tin, smoothing the mixture evenly over the bottom of the tin and pressing down with the back of a spoon. Place in the fridge to chill and harden while you make the cheesecake and strawberry layers.

4. To make a quick strawberry coulis, place the frozen strawberries and sugar in a small saucepan over a low heat. Use a potato masher to mash the strawberries into the sugar and cook for 4–5 minutes until the coulis is a thick, jam-like consistency. Set aside to cool.

5. To make the cheesecake layer, melt the cream cheese in a heatproof mixing bowl set over a pan of simmering water or in a bain-marie. Mix the cornflour with 4 tablespoons of water and add to the cream cheese. Keeping the bowl over the heat, whisk together for about 5 minutes until the mixture has thickened. Remove from the heat and add the vanilla extract and salt and sift in the icing sugar. Mix well to fully combine.

6. Assemble the cheesecake by placing the sliced strawberries evenly over the base. Pour the cream cheese mixture evenly over the strawberries then spoon over the coulis and swirl it through the cream cheese mixture, taking care not to mix it in too much. Place in the freezer to set for about 1 hour 30 minutes.

7. Halve the reserved strawberries, remove the cheesecake from the freezer and place the strawberriy halves on top. Cut the frozen cheesecake into about 12 slices. Leave at room temperature for about 5 minutes to soften a little before serving.

Raspberry & White Choc Skillet Cookie

110g (4oz) vegan butter, plus extra for greasing

1½ tsp vanilla extract

75g (2½oz) brown sugar

100g (3½oz) caster sugar

200g (7oz) plain flour

1 tsp baking powder

½ tsp bicarbonate of soda

½ tsp salt

2 tbsp vegan milk

50g (1¾oz) vegan white chocolate chips

100g (3½oz) frozen raspberries

To serve

fresh raspberries

vegan vanilla ice cream

We think this dessert needs no introduction, and was another huge hit in the office when we were running trials. This flavour combination is such a winner for us and the hot cookie dough served with cold ice cream never gets old.

1. Preheat the oven to 180°C fan/350°F/gas 6.

2. Cream together the butter, vanilla extract and both sugars using a hand-held electric whisk. Sift in the flour, baking powder, bicarb and salt and mix everything together well. Drizzle in the milk until the mixture resembles slightly sticky cookie dough (you may only need 1 tablespoon so add this slowly). Finally, fold in the white chocolate chips then the frozen raspberries.

3. Grease a 20-cm (8-inch) skillet with butter or line an 18x18-cm (7x7-inch) deep baking dish with parchment paper. Spoon the cookie mixture into the prepared skillet or dish and spread it out evenly.

4. Bake in the preheated oven for 25–30 minutes, or until lightly browned on top. If it starts to brown too quickly, cover with foil to prevent it burning.

5. Remove from the oven and leave to cool slightly for 5–10 minutes, then serve warm with a scoop of vanilla ice cream and some fresh raspberries.

CHEF'S TIP: we would highly recommend using a skillet for this recipe as it retains the heat really well and will give you those beautiful caramelised edges.

Puff Pastry Cinnamon Swirls

For the cinnamon rolls

80g (2¾oz) caster sugar

1½ tsp ground cinnamon

20g (¾oz) vegan butter

2 tbsp plain flour, for dusting

500g (1.1lb) puff pastry block

For the glaze

75g (2½oz) icing sugar

Sometimes we want the indulgence of a fluffy cinnamon roll but without all the faff, so this puff pastry version is the perfect thing to throw in the oven for a very minimal effort dessert. Most blocks of puff pastry are accidentally vegan, just be sure to check the label.

1. Preheat the oven to 180°C fan/350°F/gas 6.

2. Place the caster sugar and cinnamon in a shallow bowl and mix together to combine.

3. Gently melt the butter in a bowl in the microwave for 20 seconds or in a saucepan over a low heat.

4. Lightly dust a clean work surface with flour and roll out the puff pastry block into a large rectangle about 4mm (⅛ inch) thick. Brush the surface of the puff pastry all over with the melted butter, then sprinkle the cinnamon sugar evenly over the top; most of the sugar will sink into the melted butter.

5. With the longest edge of the rectangle facing you, roll up the pastry lengthways into a spiral then cut the pastry roll into slices 2.5cm (1 inch) thick. Lay the swirls down flat so that the spiral shape is facing upwards and use the palm of your hand to flatten down the swirls slightly, this will ensure everything cooks evenly.

6. Place the swirls on a baking sheet lined with parchment paper and bake in the preheated oven for 22–24 minutes until golden brown.

7. Meanwhile, mix the icing sugar with 1 tablespoon of water to make the glaze.

8. Remove the swirls from the oven and leave to cool for 5 minutes, then liberally drizzle over the glaze. Serve hot or cold.

CHEF'S TIP: for an even quicker dessert, swap out the block of pastry for a pre-rolled sheet.

SERVES 2 · **5 mins** · **GF**
+45 mins

Chocolate Froyo

40g (1½oz) vegan dark chocolate, broken into small pieces

200g (7oz) vegan yoghurt

80g (2¾oz) vegan condensed milk

½ tbsp vanilla extract

1 tbsp cocoa powder

2 tbsp golden syrup

a pinch of salt

We couldn't believe how easy making a vegan froyo was... and you can pretty much swap out the chocolate for any of your favourite flavours – the choice is yours!

1. Gently melt the dark chocolate in a heatproof bowl in the microwave at 20-second intervals, stirring in between to make sure the chocolate doesn't burn.

2. Place the remaining ingredients in a blender and blitz until everything is smooth and combined.

3. Add the melted dark chocolate and blend again then pour into a freezer-safe container and place in the freezer for 45 minutes.

4. When frozen, remove from the freezer and serve using an ice cream scoop.

CHEF'S TIP: the thicker vegan Greek-style yoghurts will give you an even thicker froyo.

Ultimate Shake Base

SERVES 2 · 5 mins (+10 mins) · GF

This is a super simple version of the iconic shake base that's available in our restaurants. We've included it here so you can enjoy this every day!

440ml (15fl oz) vegan milk

2 tbsp cashew butter (or any other nut butter of choice)

1 tbsp agave syrup

2 tsp chia seeds

1 tsp vanilla extract

a pinch of salt

a handful of ice cubes

1. Place all the ingredients in a blender and blitz together until smooth.

2. Pour the shake mixture into two glasses and place in the fridge for 10 minutes to thicken up (as the chia seeds sit in the fridge they will help your shake become beautifully thick).

3. Give the shakes a quick stir through before serving, chilled.

Tiramisu Shake

SERVES 2 · 10 mins (+1 hour)

One of our most popular shakes around the festive season, this is a recipe we always go back to if we want pure indulgence with a little caffeine hit.

350ml (12fl oz) strong brewed coffee

100ml (3½fl oz) vegan cream

400ml (14fl oz) vegan milk

6 bourbon biscuits

1 tsp vanilla extract

a pinch of salt

a pinch of cocoa powder

To serve

50ml (1¾fl oz) whippable vegan cream

3 tbsp vegan chocolate dessert sauce

1 tbsp cocoa powder

1. Pour the coffee into an ice cube tray and freeze for at least 1 hour, or until solid.

2. Meanwhile, place the whippable cream in a clean mixing bowl and beat with a hand-held electric whisk to firm up. Whisk for about 5 minutes until the cream has thickened into stiff peaks.

3. When the coffee ice cubes are frozen, place the remaining ingredients in a blender with three quarters of the coffee ice cubes. Blitz until smooth.

4. To serve, drizzle the chocolate dessert sauce around the inside edge of two glasses then pour in the shake mixture.

5. Add the remaining ice cubes and finish with the whipped cream and a dusting of cocoa powder.

SERVES 2–4

30 mins

+2 hours

Lemon & Peach Iced Tea Slushie

3 green tea bags

500ml (17fl oz) freshly boiled water

415g (14½oz) tin peaches in syrup, drained, syrup reserved

juice and zest of ½ lemon

2 tbsp maple syrup

To serve

fresh mint

A deliciously refreshing, pick-me-up on a hot summer's day. This is super simple to make and is perfect for a get-together with friends.

1. Place the tea bags in a heatproof container and pour over the freshly boiled water. Leave the tea to steep and cool slightly for 5 minutes.

2. Remove the tea bags and pour the liquid into an ice cube tray, then place in the freezer for at least 2 hours until ready to serve.

3. Place the tea ice cubes, 200ml (7fl oz) of the syrup from the tinned peaches and all the remaining ingredients into a blender and blend.

4. Pour into glasses and serve with a sprig of fresh mint.

CHEF'S TIP: make the ice cubes a day in advance for a really quick and convenient summer cooler.

Sauces

Sauces

Perfect Mayo Base

MAKES 600g (1.3lb) · 10 mins · GF

180ml (6fl oz) soya milk

1 tsp Dijon mustard

½ tsp salt

1 tsp agave syrup

1 tbsp white wine vinegar

500ml (17fl oz) vegetable oil

We have been making our sauces in house since 2016, so we had to include our recipe for a perfect vegan mayo base.

1. Place the soya milk, mustard, salt, agave syrup and white wine vinegar in a mixing bowl. Blitz together using a stick blender in one hand, then with your other hand slowly pour in the oil.

2. Keep blending until everything is fully emulsified and the mayo is nice and thick and glossy.

3. Enjoy this creamy mayo as it is or use it as the perfect base for the other mayo recipes in this chapter.

4. Place in an airtight storage container and keep in the fridge for up to 3 weeks.

CHEF'S TIP: use a soya milk with a high soya bean content to ensure the mayo gets super thick and glossy.

Burger Sauce

MAKES 225g (8oz) · 10 mins · GF

150g (5¼oz) Perfect Mayo Base (see above)

30g (1oz) gherkins, finely diced

2 tbsp ketchup

1 tbsp yellow mustard

1 tsp white wine vinegar

½ tsp paprika

½ tsp maple syrup

This is everyone's favourite burger sauce and the perfect accompaniment to our MLT burger (see page 80).

1. Place all the ingredients in a mixing bowl and blitz using a stick blender until the sauce is smooth, with no lumps.

2. Place in an airtight storage container and keep in the fridge for up to 3 weeks.

Veg Scrap Mayo

MAKES 250g (9oz) · 20 mins · GF

This is a great way to use up any vegetables that are past their best, or any scraps that you would otherwise throw away.

oil, for frying

½ red onion, skin on, roughly chopped

2 sticks celery, roughly chopped

4 cloves garlic, skin on

skin of 1 potato

1 tsp liquid smoke

1 tsp agave syrup

½ tsp salt

½ tsp black pepper

½ tsp chilli powder

½ tsp paprika

150g (5¼oz) Perfect Mayo Base (see opposite)

1. Heat a tablespoon of oil in a frying pan over a medium heat. Add the onion, celery, whole garlic cloves and potato skin and fry for 2 minutes. Add the liquid smoke, agave syrup and other seasonings and cook for a further 3 minutes.

2. Place the mixture in a mixing bowl and add the mayo and 50ml (1¾fl oz) water. Blitz using a stick blender until the mayo is smooth, with no lumps.

3. Place in an airtight storage container and keep in the fridge for up to 7 days.

Tangy Ranch Dip

MAKES 180g (6½ oz) · 10 mins · GF

This is the sauce used in our bestselling Crispy Chicken Vurger, the perfect balance of tangy and herby, and totally addictive!

150g (5¼oz) Perfect Mayo Base (see opposite)

1 tbsp apple cider vinegar

1 tbsp vegan milk

1 tsp lemon juice

½ tsp salt

½ tsp black pepper

½ tsp dried mixed herbs

1 tsp garlic powder

1. Place all the ingredients in a mixing bowl and stir well until fully incorporated.

2. Place in an airtight storage container and keep in the fridge for up to 3 weeks.

TANGY RANCH DIP

BURGER
SAUCE

VEG SCRAP
MAYO

MAKES 220g (8oz) · 35 mins · GF

Roasted Triple Garlic Aioli

8 cloves garlic, skin on

150g (5¼oz) Perfect Mayo Base (see page 180)

1 tsp black garlic paste

1 clove garlic, minced

1 tsp nutritional yeast flakes

1 tsp lemon juice

¼ tsp salt

¼ tsp black pepper

1. Preheat the oven to 180°C fan/350°F/gas 6.

2. Wrap the whole garlic cloves, with skin on, in foil and roast in the preheated oven for 30 minutes.

3. Meanwhile, place all the remaining ingredients in a mixing bowl and stir well until fully incorporated.

4. When the garlic has finished roasting, remove from the oven and leave until cool enough to handle then squeeze each clove out onto a chopping board. Use the back of a knife to crush the garlic cloves until they are puréed. Add to the mayo and mix well to combine.

5. Place in an airtight storage container and keep in the fridge for up to 7 days.

Buffalo Aioli

MAKES 190g (6½ oz)
5 mins
GF

150g (5¼oz) Perfect Mayo Base (see page 180)

35g (1¼oz) buffalo hot sauce

1 clove garlic, minced

1 tsp smoked paprika

a pinch of chilli powder

1. Place all the ingredients in a mixing bowl and stir well until fully incorporated.

2. Place in an airtight storage container and keep in the fridge for up to 1 month.

'Honey' Mustard Aioli

MAKES 200g (7oz)
5 mins
GF

150g (5¼oz) Perfect Mayo Base (see page 180)

1 tsp onion powder

1 tsp garlic powder

1 tbsp Dijon mustard

1 tbsp wholegrain mustard

1 tbsp maple syrup

1. Place all the ingredients in a mixing bowl and stir well until fully incorporated.

2. Place in an airtight storage container and keep in the fridge for up to 1 month.

HONEY
MUSTARD
AIOLI

BUFFALO
AIOLI

TRIPLE GARLIC
AIOLI

'Chicken' Gravy

2 tbsp vegetable oil

1 red onion, chopped

1 carrot, chopped

1 stick celery, chopped

1 leek, chopped

125g (4½oz) chestnut mushrooms, cleaned and chopped

3 cloves garlic, minced

1 tsp dried sage

1 tsp dried rosemary

1 tsp dried parsley

½ tsp dried thyme

½ tsp salt

1 tsp black pepper

1 bay leaf

2 tbsp plain flour

100ml (3½fl oz) white wine

600ml (20fl oz) vegetable stock

1 tsp Marmite

1 tsp agave syrup

1 tbsp balsamic vinegar

½ tbsp miso paste

2 tbsp nutritional yeast flakes

We are passionate about vegan chicken, and what better way to complete your Kentucky fried feast than with a rich, flavourful gravy. Perfect with our Southern-fried Nuggets (see page 106).

1. Heat the oil in a large saucepan over a medium heat. Add the chopped vegetables except the garlic and sauté for about 10 minutes until everything is golden, then add the garlic and stir through. Add the dried herbs and seasonings and fry off for about 2 minutes until fragrant. Add the flour and stir well to fully incorporate, cooking for a further minute.

2. Add the white wine to deglaze the pan, scraping the bottom of the pan with a wooden spoon to mix in any flavoursome crusty bits. Reduce the heat to low and simmer until the wine has evaporated, then add the remaining ingredients, stirring together well. Simmer for a further 10–15 minutes, or until the mix is lovely and thick.

3. Pour the gravy mix through a sieve into a bowl. Use the back of a spoon to press the mixture into the sieve to squeeze out as much flavour from the vegetables as possible. Wipe out the saucepan and pour the strained gravy back into the pan, place over a low-medium heat to bring the gravy back up to temperature.

4. Serve piping hot with your favourite vegan fried 'chicken' or freeze for up to a month and defrost and reheat whenever that gravy craving hits you!

CHEF'S TIP: this freezes really well in an ice cube tray, so you can simply take a cube or two out at a time to defrost and serve as a dip with vegan fried 'chicken' – delicious.

Peri-peri Sauce

6 tbsp vegetable oil

1 bird's eye chilli, chopped

1 red chilli, chopped

½ red onion, chopped

4 cloves garlic, chopped

1 tsp dried sage

1 tsp dried oregano

1 tsp smoked paprika

1 tsp salt

½ tsp black pepper

juice and zest of ½ lemon

130g (4¾oz) roasted red peppers

½ tbsp white wine vinegar

1. Heat 2 tablespoons of the oil in a frying pan over a medium heat and fry the chopped ingredients for 10 minutes, or until softened. Add the herbs and spices and fry for a further minute, then remove from the heat.

2. Place the mixture in a beaker that will accommodate a stick blender. Add the lemon juice and zest, roasted red peppers, white wine vinegar and the remaining 4 tablespoons of oil.

3. Blitz until the sauce is smooth, with no lumps.

4. Store in a clean airtight storage jar the fridge until ready to use, and top with a little oil after each use to keep the sauce fresh. The sauce can be kept refrigerated for up to 7 days.

CHEF'S TIP: feel free to use more or less chilli depending on your spice tolerance!

MAKES 400g (14oz) · 15 mins · GF

'Bacon' & Onion Jam

oil, for frying

1 red onion, finely chopped

4 cloves garlic, finely chopped

160g (5½oz) vegan 'bacon' lardons

4 tbsp brown sugar

2 tbsp balsamic vinegar

2 tbsp soy sauce

1 tsp paprika

a pinch of black pepper

1. Heat a splash of oil in a frying pan over a medium heat. Add the onion and sauté for about 5 minutes until softened.

2. Add the garlic and 'bacon' lardons and fry for another 2–3 minutes, until the 'bacon' is slightly crispy.

3. Add the remaining ingredients along with 5 tablespoons of water and stir through until the mixture is thick and caramelised. This should take about 10 minutes.

4. Store in a clean airtight storage jar and use within 5 days.

CHEF'S TIP: leave to caramelise for longer depending on how thick you want your jam to be.

PERI-PERI
SAUCE

'BACON' &
ONION JAM

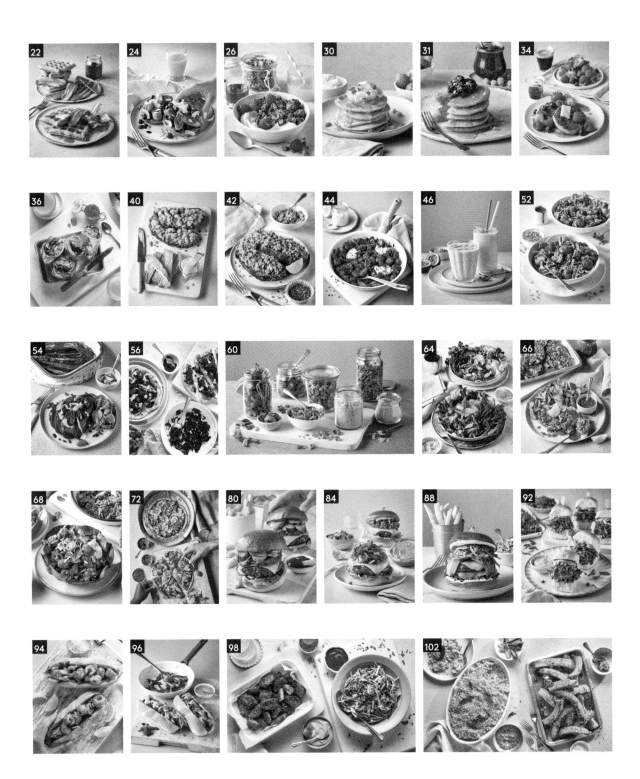

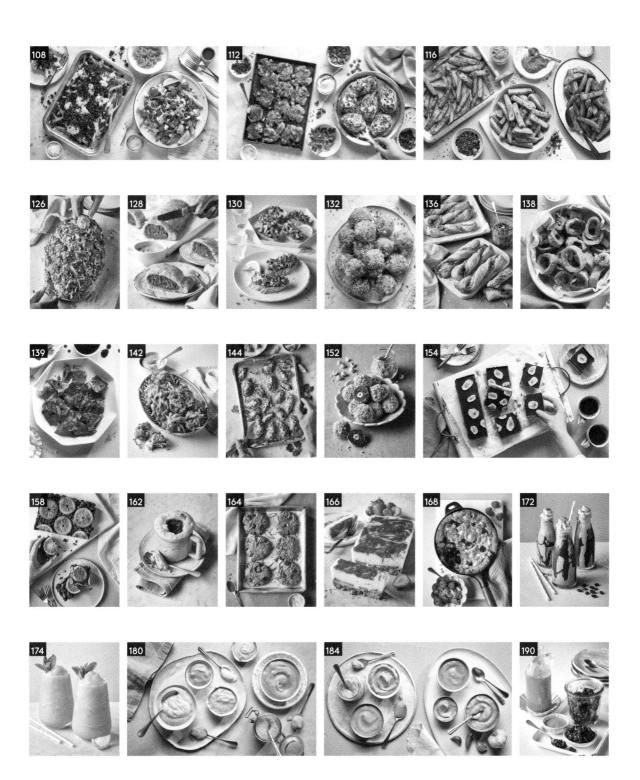

Index

Page numbers in *italic* refer to the photographs

Index

Index

Index

Index

Index

Index

Index

Index

Index

Index

Index

Acknowledgements

We are incredibly grateful to many people for making this dream a reality.

First and foremost, our incredible team...

Starting with Elly Smart and Carolyn Mwarazi. Elly first joined our team back in 2019 and her dedication, passion and true talent is here for everyone to see and taste for themselves. Elly spent a very long time pulling together a combination of recipes from years gone by, brand new creations and some team favourites too. Supported by Carolyn, who joined our team in 2021, her eye for detail and serious love of creating delicious food is extremely inspiring. Thank you both from the bottom of our hearts for your time and dedication in making this recipe book come to life. It was not easy, especially when nobody in our team knew what was going on and we were trying to open a new store at the same time – but we are so proud of everything we have overcome as a team to make this a reality. You are both incredible and we are so grateful to have you driving our culinary innovation every day.

To Paula Nogueira and Denise Fernandes, our unbelievably talented creative team, who have been non-stop making sure the design aesthetic of the book, the imagery and the overall vision came to life. Not only this book, but everything you see with our brand, from online, to our restaurants, to supermarket shelves – it's all a direct result of your amazing skills. Where would we be without you, your talent, your vision, and execution? Simply, thank you!

To chef Gaz Oakley. Our long-term friend and incredible investor, Gaz is an extremely inspirational and talented chef. How he puts certain flavours together and makes them the best dish ever is beyond our understanding. Thank you, Gaz, for your support from day one and for contributing with your incredible and seriously delicious recipes.

To our photographer Simon Smith, who we have worked with since 2018 after being introduced by Gaz. With a career that spans decades in the photography world, we just knew Simon would be the best photographer to work with on this book.

A very dear thank you to Pippa Leon, who we worked with for the very first time on this book as our food stylist. We are truly thankful we met, as Pippa made this project on set a total breeze; we are beyond grateful to have worked with you.

Thank you to the team at HarperCollins for all of your help and support and for coming to us with the original plan to create this book. Lydia and Sarah, you have been the most wonderful team to work with and have been instrumental in bringing this idea and project to life. Thank you for your belief in our brand, for your vision and for putting up with us along the way.

Thank you to our whole team, past and present – you have all contributed immeasurably to making this brand what it is today and we're so grateful for your phenomenal efforts every day.

Thank you to our investors, our family and our friends who have shown undeniable support right from the beginning and throughout our journey.

Thank you to you; our customers. Without your passion and love for our brand, and your constant support every day, we simply wouldn't be where we are today.

We are so grateful that we have been able to bring this book to life and hope it will become a staple recipe book in homes across the world.

A big thank you all round,
Rachel and Neil

HarperCollins*Publishers*
1 London Bridge Street
London SE1 9GF

www.harpercollins.co.uk

HarperCollins*Publishers*
Macken House, 39/40 Mayor Street Upper
Dublin 1, D01 C9W8, Ireland

First published by HarperCollins*Publishers* 2023

1 3 5 7 9 10 8 6 4 2

A catalogue record of this book is available from the British Library

ISBN 978-0-00-854596-3

Photographer: Simon Smith
Food Stylist: Pippa Leon
Prop Stylist: Jenny Iggelden

Printed and bound by GPS, Slovenia

MIX
Paper from
responsible sources
FSC™ C007454
FSC
www.fsc.org

This book is produced from independently certified FSC™ paper
to ensure responsible forest management.

For more information visit: www.harpercollins.co.uk/green

WHEN USING KITCHEN APPLIANCES PLEASE ALWAYS FOLLOW THE
MANUFACTURER'S INSTRUCTIONS